THE
OLDEST
FOODS
ON EARTH

JOHN NEWTON is a freelance writer, journalist and novelist. He writes on food, eating, travel, farming and associated environmental issues. His most recent books are *Grazing: The Ramblings and Recipes of a Man Who Gets Paid to Eat* (2010) and *A Savage History: Whaling in the Pacific and Southern Oceans* (2013). In 2005 he won the Gold Ladle for Best Food Journalist in the World Food Media Awards.

THE
OLDEST
FOODS
ON EARTH

A HISTORY OF AUSTRALIAN NATIVE FOODS
WITH RECIPES

JOHN NEWTON

NEWSOUTH

A NewSouth book

Published by
NewSouth Publishing
University of New South Wales Press Ltd
University of New South Wales
Sydney NSW 2052
AUSTRALIA
newsouthpublishing.com

National Library of Australia
Cataloguing-in-Publication entry

Creator: Newton John, author.
Title: The Oldest Foods on Earth: A history of Australian native foods, with recipes / John Newton.
ISBN: 9781742234373 (paperback)
       9781742242262 (ebook)
       9781742247632 (ePDF)
Notes: Includes index.
Subjects: Natural foods – Australia – History.
       Wild plants, Edible – Australia – History.
       Cooking, Australian.
       Cooking (Natural foods) – Australia.
Dewey Number: 641.302

Design Josephine Pajor-Markus
Cover design Blue Cork
Cover images © Oliver Strewe/Corbis
Printer Griffin

All reasonable efforts were taken to obtain permission to use copyright material reproduced in this book, but in some cases copyright could not be traced. The author welcomes information in this regard.

This book is printed on paper using fibre supplied from plantation or sustainably managed forests.

UNSW
AUSTRALIA

CONTENTS

INTRODUCTION

When was the last time you seared a kangaroo fillet and served it with a pepperberry sauce? Have you ever eaten quandong? Riberries? Magpie goose? Did you know that before we arrived in 1788 the Aboriginal people of the tropical North chose from among 750 different plant and animal foods? Did you know that Australian native rices (*Oryza rufipogon* and *O. meridionalis*) were an abundant and widespread resource in floodplains across monsoonal Australia and were harvested and consumed by the First People for thousands of years? Only now are they being cultivated for wider consumption.

This is a book about Australian food. Not the food that European Australians cooked from ingredients they brought with them, but the unique flora and fauna that nourished the Aboriginal peoples of this land for over 50 000 years. Indeed, it is because European Australians have hardly ever touched these foods for over 200 years that I am writing this book. The reason we virtually ignored the foods that were here when we came is part of this story. But only a part. The real story is that these foods are, finally, beginning to be used by home and professional chefs. It's somewhat tentative – especially in the home – but it's a start. There's a long way to go yet.

The first time I ate kangaroo was in 1993 at a long-gone restaurant called Oasis Seros. I was reviewing the restaurant for *The Sydney Morning Herald Good Food Guide*. The chef was Phillip Searle and the dish was Kangaroo with Pickled Beetroot. I have never forgotten it. The combination of the lightly seared roo with the complex acidity of the sauce was, for this diner, unforgettable. For this book, I made contact with Phillip, and he very kindly gave me the recipe, which you'll find at the end of this introduction (see page xvii).

In more than 200 years of occupation of this continent, European Australians have turned their backs on the vast majority of the foods the Indigenous people have been eating for more than 50 000 years; ignored their sage and intricate management of the environment and its abundant foods; overlaid an alien system of agriculture which began the process of ecological imbalance the continent now finds itself in; and began exporting back to Europe the exotic foodstuffs they planted and raised. And, for around 150 years, stuck stubbornly to the diet of the first settlers.

In short, we lived on and not *in* this continent. We did not put down roots and did not see, as American food historian Waverley Root asserted, that 'food is a function of the soil, for which reason every country has the food naturally fit for it.' Every country, that is, except Australia.

As I was writing this I flicked across to the *Sydney Morning Herald* website. There was a clickbait headline:

'Where to taste the world's best cuisines.' Alright, I'll bite, tell me: Japan, Peru, France, Spain, Morocco, Argentina, Taiwan and Italy. There appears to be something missing. And it's not the cultural cringe, though we're good at that.

Later I'll discuss those foods breathlessly referred to as 'superfoods' in the health pages of our glossies. Why do they always come from somewhere else, some usually exotic place? The acai berry from Amazonia; the goji berry from the Ningxia Hui region in north central China or the Xinjiang Uighur region in far northern China; quinoa from Peru and Bolivia. If those imports are superfoods, the foods that have been growing here for thousands of years, Australian native foods, foods that we've virtually ignored for the 200-plus years we've been here, are super-duperfoods.

In this book, I deal with what pioneer native foods chef Jean-Paul Bruneteau calls 'food racism', the kind that has, in the past, played its part in the rejection of these foods because they were Aboriginal foods. It is only one of the many kinds of racism directed against the Aboriginal people, even today. My own belief is that non-Indigenous Australians must accept that the original inhabitants have carefully stewarded this land for the entire time they have lived here, and have the oldest unbroken culture in the world, before that racism – culinary and otherwise – will disappear.

And there's something else really puzzling about our rejecting and ignoring the foods that grow here.

Australia has absorbed, with minimal racial problems, more nationalities than just about any country on earth. And as the philosopher and historian Anthony Corones has shown, Australia is not just a multicultural society, but a multiculinary one. As pioneer native Australian food restaurateur Jennice Kersh once said, 'We have embraced multicultural food more than any country in the world. Australia jumped in there and hugged it all. They'd go to a Thai restaurant – any kind of restaurant – and have no fear.' We'll happily eat boat noodle soup – with beef blood stirred through it – or stinking tofu, but not kangaroo. Which dispenses with the theory of neophobia – fear of the new: in this instance, new food.

There's something else going on here in the rejection of native foods. Moving on from that rejection can only be good for Australian culture.

A study carried out in Malaysia concludes by noting that 'When two or more ethnic groups share foodways, they become closer.' The report also suggests that when different ethnic groups share food, it strengthens social bonding and alliances among communities and ethnic groups – an important consideration in multiculinary and multicultural Malaysia, a country often riven by racial and ethnic conflict.

I do believe that Australian multiculinarity – accepting the food of 'the others', eating our neighbours' food – has helped us ease our way into what is generally a remarkable multicultural stability.

If the acceptance of foods can help Australians become more tolerant of new arrivals to this land, surely, then, it can do the same with the food of those who were here long before we arrived. Food is more than nourishment. Food is culture; food *shapes* culture; food binds us together and forces us apart. In the same way, accepting the food of this land, which we are only just beginning to do after almost 230 years, will, I believe, contribute towards what I call culinary reconciliation.

There are also environmental advantages of eating more of those foods that have adapted to the climates of the land, which for the most part don't require chemical interventions to protect them from weeds and insect predators. The same goes for the native animals: they too have adapted to live lightly on the land. This could be the most compelling reason of all.

There are signs that cultural change is happening. More generally, I'd point to the success of films like *The Sapphires* and *Charlie's Country*, and ABC television shows like *Redfern Now* and *Black Comedy*. I simply can't imagine these shows – especially *Black Comedy* – appearing on mainstream Australian television, even the ABC, even ten years ago. And, slowly, it's happening with food. A new generation of young Australian chefs who don't carry the racial baggage of the past are using native Australian ingredients. Chinese Australian chef Kylie Kwong has added lilly pilly (riberries), wallaby tail, quandongs and saltbush to her menu. Visiting English molecular chef Heston Blumenthal incorporated lemon myrtle and pepperberries in a range he developed with a local supermarket. Both home cooks and restaurant chefs are picking riberries from street plantings of lilly pilly, foraging for warrigal greens and experimenting with kangaroo. Sales of native ingredients are increasing. The ingredients are a-changing.

And about bloody time.

A NOTE ON TERMINOLOGY

While I prefer the term First People, I will be using the words Aborigine (noun, sparingly) and Aboriginal (adjective) to describe those people who have occupied, farmed and cared for this land for over 50000 years. While these words are a little old-fashioned – especially Aborigine – they seem to be accepted by the community. I'll alternate Aboriginal with Indigenous, a term with mixed acceptance, but one that's here to stay.

Unlike New Zealand's Māori people, in Australia there are some 500 nations, with many different terms for each other – Koori in New South Wales, Murri in Queensland, Nyoongar in southern Western Australia, Nunga in southern South Australia, Palawa in Tasmania and Yolngu or Yolnu in north-eastern Arnhem Land being just a few. Even deciding what to call the original inhabitants of this country is complex. It has been estimated that before the colonisers arrived there were some 700 language groups, of which 250 have been recorded.

In spite of this, as Bill Gammage shows in his magisterial book *The Biggest Estate on Earth*, there was a cohesive farming and land management plan across the entire continent, or 'estate' as Gammage calls it. How was this done? Gammage writes, 'Although comprising many ways of maintaining land, and managers mostly unknown to each other, this vast area was governed by a single religious philosophy, called in English the Dreaming.'

I will refer often to Bill Gammage's book. His research completely destroys the myth of the 'wandering savages.' He carefully and thoroughly shows the impact that the Indigenous people of this country had on the land, and shows, as Henry Reynolds writes in the foreword, 'the scale of Aboriginal land management [and] the intelligence, skill and inherited knowledge which informed it'. If this book does no more than lead its reader to Gammage, it will have fulfilled its purpose.

The terms that I come across often in conversation with Indigenous Australians and those who work with them are Whitefella and Blackfella. I like them very much. They differentiate without discriminating. But they don't work so well on the page.

And then there are the terms used by the Blackfellas to indicate Whitefellas. There are a few: *Balanda* in Arnhem Land and the Northern Territory; *Gubba* or *Gub* in south-eastern Australia; *Wajala* in Western

Australia; and *Walypala* in parts of northern Australia.

While we now know that to label the Aboriginal people as hunter-gatherers is inadequate to describe the complex and time-honoured ways in which they managed the entire country, I will use this term as shorthand from time to time, as it continues to be used in the literature to the present day.

At the beginning of this Introduction, I wrote 'European Australians have turned their backs on the vast majority of the foods the Indigenous people have been eating for more than 50 000 years.' You will all be aware that there are, of course, Indigenous foods we have always eaten, for example oysters, crabs, rock crayfish, yabbies and marron, and all the fish that swim around us. As the chef Tony Bilson reminds us, these fish include many of those used in the French dish bouillabaisse: rascasse (here known as red rock cod), daurade (similar to snapper) and mullet. These were all familiar to the new settlers (although, as I show later in the book, the snapper was often shunned as not good enough for the dinner table). And there were familiar game birds – varieties of duck and quail, for example.

But outside the familiar are an estimated 6000 edible plants, including 2400 fruiting trees in south-eastern Queensland alone, 2000 truffles or subterranean mush-rooms, and a number of game birds and mammals, including the kangaroo, which is still scarcely eaten domestically. There is much still to explore in the unfa-miliar, and this book will explore at least some of them.

The questions of when the first humans arrived on the Australian continent, and whether there was one arrival or several, are still being disputed. Without getting into the multiple arrival argument, I'll briefly examine the claims around dating.

Archaeological evidence indicates human habitation at the upper Swan River in western Australia about 40000 years ago. Tasmania, which was then connected to the continent by a land bridge, was inhabited at least 30,000 years ago. Analysis of sediments at two grave sites at Lake Mungo confirms that Australia is the site of the world's oldest known burial with red ochre and the oldest cremation, thus providing additional evidence that early humans first reached Australia about 50000 years ago.

The anatomy of the very first physical records of the humans found at these gravesites also complements this picture. We see a morphology (a branch of biology dealing with the form and structure of organisms) in the remains of what have come to be known as Mungo Man and Mungo Woman that would not look out of place in Aboriginal Australian populations today. Astonishingly, Mungo Man and Woman are fully modern people in every sense of the word, and indeed represent some of the earliest modern human remains within the whole Australian–Asian region. Europe at this time was still the domain of the Neanderthals.

There have been claims that some sites are up to 60000 years old, but these claims are not generally accepted. Neither is the evidence from south-eastern Australia, which suggests an increase in fire activity dating from around 120 000 years ago, which has been interpreted as evidence of human activity.

At the time of writing it seems reasonable to adopt 'over 50 000 years' as the most generally accepted dating of the arrival of humans on the Australian continent.

Finally, details of all books, papers and websites mentioned in the text can be found in the Bibliography.

PHILLIP SEARLE

....

KANGAROO WITH PICKLED BEETROOT

I ate this dish at Oasis Seros while reviewing it for the Sydney Morning Herald Good Food Guide *in 1993 (review published in the 1994 edition), and have never forgotten it. JN*

200 g of kangaroo tenderloin per person
enough peanut oil to marinate the kangaroo in, with
    ground black pepper, star anise, orange rind and a few
    drops of coconut vinegar added
small amount of game or veal stock
1 tsp fresh horseradish (if in season), pureed in a small
    amount of coconut vinegar

Tomato pickle
(this makes more than you will need for the recipe)
1 tbsp black mustard seeds
250 ml malt vinegar
15 cloves garlic
200 g fresh ginger, chopped
250 ml peanut oil
3 tbsp cumin seeds
1 tbsp ground turmeric
2 kg peeled, seeded, ripe tomatoes

Pickled beetroot
3 medium-sized beetroot
enough peanut oil to rub them generously with
4 cracked star anise
500 g grated palm sugar
200 ml lime juice
600 ml coconut vinegar
100 ml peanut oil
fish sauce, to taste

1. Start marinating the kangaroo a day ahead. Put it in a bowl with the peanut oil, ground black pepper, star anise, orange rind and a few drops of coconut vinegar. Cover the bowl and leave in the fridge.
2. Soak the black mustard seeds in the malt vinegar overnight. To make the tomato pickle, first dry roast the black mustard seeds until they begin to pop.
3. Toast the cumin seeds then grind in a mortar and

pestle. Make a paste by pureeing the mustard seeds with the garlic cloves, ginger and peanut oil. Sauté this in a braising pan until it begins to colour. Add the cumin and the turmeric, and cook for 5 minutes.

4. Add the grated palm sugar and cook until it dissolves. Add the tomatoes and cook a further half hour. Pour into sterilised jars. Set aside till they cool, then refrigerate.

5. To make the pickled beetroot, rub the beetroot with the peanut oil and place them in a roasting tray with the star anise. Cover the tray with foil and bake the beetroot until they are cooked – that is, softened. The pan should have a residue of beetroot juice and oil. Strain the juices and reserve.

6. Peel the beetroot (the skin will rub off if they're cooked). Make a pickle by first mixing the grated palm sugar, lime juice, coconut vinegar and peanut oil, plus the reserved pan juices. Add fish sauce to taste, as you would salt. Bring the pickling mixture to the boil, then allow it to cool. While they are hot, add the beetroot to the pickling mixture.

7. Remove the kangaroo from the marinade. Sear over a very hot flame on a hotplate, or in a skillet, on all sides for about 2 minutes. Optionally, flame it with rice wine. Rest it for ten minutes, catching the juices.

8. To assemble the dish, slice the beetroot into slices 1.5 cm thick, and put in a pan (the skillet you cooked the kangaroo in, if you used one). Add a tablespoon of the beetroot pickling mixture and three heaped

tablespoons of tomato pickle. Heat this through.

9. Add the juices from the kangaroo and a small amount of game or veal stock. Taste, and adjust seasoning if necessary.

10. Right at the end, add the fresh horseradish pureed in coconut vinegar (do not heat it after adding this). Place the beetroot and sauce on a plate and the (now sliced) kangaroo on top, and drizzle any further juices from slicing the kangaroo over it.

Phillip Searle is one of the must influential of Modern Australian chefs, through his restaurants Possums in Adelaide and Oasis Seros in Sydney and his long association with the Symposium of Australian Gastronomy.

1

BEFORE THE BOATS

Tasmannia lanceolata

They were the most healthy people I have ever seen
… they were literally glowing with health – not an
ounce of superfluous fat. They were extremely fit.

Founding doctor of the Pintupi Homelands Health Service
Dr David Scrimgeour on seeing the last of the Pintupi people
walk out of the desert in 1984

In 1688, William Dampier was the first Englishman to explore parts of Australia, to have contact with the Indigenous people and to write about the experience. On his return to England in 1691, he wrote a book, *New Voyage Around the World*, which was published in 1697. He was less than kind – or accurate – in his judgement of the people he had come across there: 'The Inhabitants of this Country are the miserablest

People in the World ... setting aside their Humane Shape, they differ but little from Brutes.' As for their diet, he wrote: 'There is neither herb, root, pulse, nor any sort of grain for them to eat that we saw; nor any sort of bird or beast that they can catch, having no instruments wherewithal to do so.'

Dampier was the first but certainly not the last to overlook the intricate patchwork of farming and land-care techniques of the original inhabitants of this land. Neither he nor most of those who followed him saw evidence of farming in the European sense – or rather, as we will see, some did but suppressed what they saw – so they surmised that these people were 'ignorant savages'. Dampier had an excuse – he wasn't here for long – but Darwin should have known better, when he called them 'a set of harmless savages wandering about without knowing where they shall sleep at night, and gaining their livelihood by hunting in the woods'. While conceding that a group of Aboriginal people that he had encountered were 'good humoured and pleasant' and that several of their remarks 'manifested considerable acuteness', Darwin deplored the fact that 'They will not ... cultivate the ground, or build houses and remain stationary, or even take the trouble of tending a flock of sheep when given to them.'

Historian William Gammage comments that 'the people of 1788 spent more time each year managing land than Darwin [did] in a lifetime.' We have learnt, thanks to the work of historians and authors like Gammage, Eric Rolls and Bruce Pascoe, that the entire country was carefully and thoroughly farmed in a manner that left the land and its bounty in balance and abundance for at least 50 000 years.

They reared possums, emus, dingos and cassowaries; they penned young pelican chicks and let parent birds fatten them. They carried fish and crayfish stock across the country. There were duck nets on the rivers with sinkers and floats, and fishing nets of European quality, with the mesh and knot varied to suit their prey, placed in the right waters. In 1839, the explorer Thomas Mitchell wrote:

> Many fish weirs were seen and one could not help being struck with the ingenuity displayed in their construction, on one creek we were surprised to find what looked like the commencement of work for a line of tramway. There were sapling sleepers about eight feet long in length and various thicknesses laid a few feet apart for at least half a mile. The work must have been done by natives but am quite at a loss to understand their motive.

It is significant, in contemplating the relationship of the Aboriginal people to the colonisers, that he did not think to ask. As Gammage writes, Aboriginal farmers 'burnt, tilled, planted, transplanted, watered, irrigated, weeded, thinned, cropped, stored and traded'. We have been shown what the first settlers missed:

that they were farmers in every sense but one – they did not put livestock behind fences. They didn't need to. The livestock were directed to the hunters by the judicious use of fire or by 'game drives', the employment of nets up to 50 feet (about 15 metres) long and kilometres of brush fences to drive game (kangaroos in the main) to the hunters. The original inhabitants of this land, unlike those who came later, worked *with* their environment, not against it.

But did the first settlers 'miss' evidence of Indigenous civilisation, or was knowledge of it deliberately suppressed? Bruce Pascoe's *Dark Emu* makes the case for suppression. Take the 'humpie' that was supposed to be the sole dwelling of Indigenous Australians: a couple of pieces of bark held up by sticks, the rudimentary dwelling of the Aboriginal warrior of my childhood imagination. One of the arguments advanced to justify European overlooking of Indigenous farming practices was that there were no dwellings: no dwelling, no fences, therefore no agriculture.

Pascoe tells of the astonishment of the late ABC broadcaster Alan Saunders on interviewing the authors of *The Encyclopedia of Australian Architecture* and discovering that the first chapter was devoted to Aboriginal architecture. As Pascoe writes, 'he wondered at the depth of Australian scholarship and education which had allowed Australians to remain ignorant of this aspect of our national culture.' Yet references to elaborate houses and villages are common. Pascoe notes, for example, that the Australian poet Dame Mary Gilmore 'reported her uncles saying that 5000 people lived around the Brewarrina fish traps.' And that Sturt reported a prosperous town of 1000 on the banks of the Darling, and writer Alice Duncan-Kemp claimed 3000 lived on Farrar's Lagoon, not far from Brewarrina.

Pascoe suggests this suppression was deliberate. Why was knowledge of sophisticated dwellings, such as the large structure in a settlement south-west of Lake Blanche in South Australia, described as 'very warm and comfortable', and 'capable of holding thirty to forty people', kept from official accounts? Because, Pascoe believes, such knowledge would get in the way of the main game: taking over the land for cultivation and the running of stock. If the local people were acknowledged as the skilled agriculturalists they were, it would have been difficult to trample all over them. This 'underestimation of indigenous achievement' writes Pascoe, 'was a deliberate tactic of British colonialism.'

If what Dampier wrote, and many other commentators more or less substantiated, were true, and the first people were 'the miserablest People in the World' and ate 'neither herb, root, pulse ... nor any sort of bird or beast that they can catch' because they had 'no instruments wherewithal to do so', they would have presented a wretched spectacle.

And although, for obvious reasons, we have no photographs of Aboriginal people before 1788, the drawings, paintings and later photographs show us a remarkably healthy population: slim, well-muscled and lithe. That is because on the whole, drought notwithstanding, they ate remarkably well from a varied diet of wild, native Australian foods. And these foods, as I will outline later in this book, were extraordinarily high in nutrients. In the Western Desert, the Aboriginal people chose from a seasonal menu of 150 different foods a year. In the tropical north, that figure jumps to 750 a year. We know this from accounts by anthropologists and others in the field who lived with them and carefully recorded what they ate, how they ate it and often how they caught or gathered it.

By contrast, the average European Australian today will choose from between fifty and a hundred foods a year, while largely ignoring even the (European imposed) seasonality of food.

One further important observation: when Europeans arrived in this country, not only did they bring their own flora and fauna, and their own agricultural methods – they also imposed the seasons of the northern hemisphere. Australia is a vast country, stretching from the tropics to the temperate zones. The four seasons of Europe do not begin to describe the variations across this vast land. But over 50 000 years, the original inhabitants have adopted seasons based upon acute observation of their country.

THE WESTERN DESERT

Between 1966 and 1967, anthropologist Richard A. Gould lived with and then reported on the food and food gathering practices of a group of thirteen Nyatunyatjara (alternate English spelling Ngaatjatjarra) people in the harsh climate of the Gibson Desert, north of Warburton, around 1500 kilometres north-west of Perth. At the time, the Western Desert was one of the last regions of the world to support groups of people living entirely on the uncultivated resources of the land. The Aboriginal settlement of the Western Desert represented possibly the most marginal example of permanent human occupation in the world, and one of the most extreme places where hunting-gathering took place. Gould and his wife (extensive research has failed to unearth her name) spent almost a year with this nomadic group. He described his purpose as studying the 'living archaeology' of these people, knowing that the days of their hunting-gathering existence were numbered. He later recorded their physical degradation when they drifted into townships.

Gould observed that the diet of the Nyatunyatjara was primarily vegetarian and at least 90 per cent of the time females provided 95 per cent of the food for the group. Men hunted constantly but had limited success, as game was only plentiful after rains. Although large game was rarely caught, a regular supply of small game contributed 9 per cent of their diet by weight. Gould mentions a total of thirty-eight edible plant species and forty-seven named varieties of meat. But on the day he describes at the opening of his book *Yiwara: Foragers of the Australian Desert*, he writes that 'as on most days, the hunt has been poor, but the collecting successful.' The only meat available was a goanna, which was roasted, cut in half and shared among the two male hunters' families by being roasted, and 'mashed' between two flat stones into a paste after the intestines were first discarded and the organs given to the hunter as his due. This paste of flesh, skin and bone provided a mouthful of food for each member of the group.

Aside from the rare treat of kangaroo or emu, other small game like the blue-tongue lizard and edible grubs provide the majority of protein, along with – at the time Gould was writing – rabbits and feral cats, which would not, of course, have been on the menu pre-1788.

On this day the women gathered two plant foods: kampurarpa, a small green tomato-like fruit (from the *Solanum* genus, as is the tomato) and ngaru, another small green tomato-like *Solanum*. Both were mashed into a paste, then eaten fresh as the paste or rolled into large balls which could be dehydrated and stored until wanted.

This was not a particularly good food day, as Gould's visit coincided with the last months of a severe drought.

He noted that while 'the people are generally strong and basically quite healthy they sometimes do show signs of deficiency', particularly the children, all of whom in his group display 'strikingly swollen bellies'. He attributes this, perhaps correctly, to protein deficiency. The disease is called by western medicine kwashiorkor. The people themselves called this condition nungkumunu, and 'proudly' show Gould the stretch marks left by this condition as evidence of 'the rigors of their childhood'. That they appear to have recovered from the affliction points towards it being minor, and a result of food shortages following drought. Even such harsh conditions were better than life post–European invasion: an estimated population of 314 500 was reduced to around 16 000 by the 1930s.

THE CENTRE

Just 1000 kilometres east is Arrernte (Aranda) country. While no Richard Gould has documented the Arrernte people's hunting and gathering, Eastern Arrernte woman Margaret-Mary Turner has published in a book, *Arrernte Foods: Foods from Central Australia*, an inventory of local foods and methods of preparing them which would have comprised the diet before 1788. She begins with honey-like foods, which include bush honey, nectar and edible gums, one of which is witchetty bush gum. Turner says, 'when the flowers start to fall, it comes out through the bark and forms in lumps … you can make it into a lump on a little stick, like a lolly.' Then there's the honey ant, which is found in the ground in Mulga country. 'You don't swallow them, you put them on your tongue and bite on the abdomen and suck the honey from it.' And there is also honey from stingless native bees.

Next, Turner lists thirty-eight foods from plants (the same number as Gould's assay of the Gibson Desert), including the wild orange, quandong, wild fig, two bush tomatoes and the bush banana fruit, flower, leaves and root. 'You can eat the bush bananas when they are small or full-grown ... You can cook bush bananas in hot earth, or they can be eaten raw when young.' The flowers 'hang in clusters and can also be eaten. You can even eat the plant itself': the root can be eaten raw or cooked. Tim Low, Australian biologist and author of *Wild Food Plants of Australia*, also records this plant, but as the native potato. Four edible seeds are listed and eleven edible grubs, caterpillars and other insects. Turner reminds us that non-Aborigines use the name witchetty grub for any edible grubs, but the witchetty grub proper is found only in the witchetty bush. Cicadas are also eaten. Most of these grubs and insects are cooked in the coals first.

There are fourteen listings under meat and other food from animals, and these include the obvious, like the goanna, bearded dragon, carpet snake (Turner remarks that one reptile 'feeds lots of people'), kangaroo, rock wallaby, euro and possum, of which Turner says 'they taste really sweet, especially the milk guts [intestines, the same as Southern American chitlins], but nowadays they are few and far between.' The crested pigeon was another prized game bird, as were the galah and the budgerigar. Of the budgerigar she writes: 'they are eaten when they are newly hatched … You cook a whole lot of them in hot earth and when they are cooked, you pull the guts out and eat the bird. Some people remove the head before eating the bird, others eat it with the head because they like the taste.'

It is doubtful that baby budgerigar will ever appear on European menus.

The last entry in Turner's book is for water, which, as in the Gibson Desert, is a scarce and crucial element. She lists soakage water (artesian water), water from tree roots, and water from tree hollows. 'Survival' she writes, 'depends on knowing how to find water.'

THE TROPICAL NORTH

Aboriginal groups throughout the tropical north of Australia have the same seasonal cycle as the Yolnu (the Aboriginal group of north-east Arnhem Land, sometimes spelt Yolngu). Aboriginal groups in other parts of Australia have a seasonal cycle based on local seasonal indicators, such as changes in wind direction, animal behaviour, and plant flowering and fruiting. The delineation of these seasons and the foods associated with them is laid out by Stephen Davis in his book

Man of All Seasons. Davis, an anthropologist, like Gould lived with the local people with his family for three years and shared their daily routine. During that time, he documented the Yolnu seasons:

» Dhuludur: the pre-wet season in October–November
» Bärra'mirri: the growth season in December–January
» Mayaltha: the flowering season in February–March
» Midawarr: the fruiting season in March–April, including
» Ngathangamakulingamirri, the two week harvest season in April
» Dharratharramirri: the early dry season in May–July, including
» Burrugumirri, the time of the birth of sharks and stingrays – three weeks in July–August
» Rarrandharr: the main dry season in August–October.

The range of foodstuffs available to the Yolnu people across these seasons is remarkable, making our European choices appear skimpy. Even in the pre-wet season, Dhuludur, one of the least prolific, there is much to choose from.

Native grape, long and round yam, the new growth of the finger bean and the giant waterlily. As the waterholes shrink early in the season, magpie geese flock to the remaining water making them easy prey for hunters. When they begin to fill, the whistling duck, Pacific black duck and radjah shelduck all come home to build their nests to breed which means they are fat.

The Yolnu people place edible plants in two groups: *ngatha*, which (in the main) bear their crops underground, and *borum*, fruit. The main sources of *ngatha* in the monsoon forest at Midawarr, the fruiting season, are the round yam, the finger bean and the pink lily. In the open woodland they are:

» long yam
» cocky apple
» grass potato
» native grape
» bush carrot
» native rosella
» flat swamp potato
» waxflower
» lily
» zamia palm
» yellow-faced bean.

Borum found in the monsoon forest include:

» fire vine
» wild gooseberry

» native pomegranate
» billabong tree
» aspirin tree
» sandpaper fig
» Polynesian arrowroot
» jungle currant
» tall rod grass
» plum
» broom berry.

And in the open woodland:

» wild passionfruit
» paper berry
» billy goat plum (a.k.a. Kakadu plum)
» wild cucumber
» red jungle berry
» aspirin tree
» tall rod grass.

And edible flowers in the waterholes include:

» fringed lily
» creek lily
» giant water lily
» blue water lily
» mangrove fern.

Animal foods include the agile wallaby, blue-tongue lizard and three turtles, the northern long-necked turtle, the northern red-faced turtle and the flat-backed turtle. At night, dugong are hunted. Of course, myriad fish are available, as are shellfish, crabs and, as the next season, the early dry season, approaches, the black-lipped oyster fattens.

SOUTH-EASTERN AUSTRALIA

This takes in the area from present day Brisbane to Adelaide, and inland to Broken Hill. Before 1788, it represented ninety to one hundred language groups.

In the southernmost parts of this region – southern New South Wales and Victoria – winters were cold, and elaborately decorated possum skin cloaks were made and worn after the possums themselves were roasted in the hot ashes. The skins were pegged out, dried, and incised to render them more flexible and also to mark them with intricate designs. They were sewn together with needles and thread made from the dried sinews of kangaroo tails. In *Dark Emu*, Bruce Pascoe writes: 'the manufacture of cloaks, hats, shoes and skirts is a study on its own but once again … is waiting for Australians to fully appreciate Aboriginal achievements.'

Kangaroos and emus were hunted or caught in pit traps. Birds, including brush turkey, were caught by a hunter with a slip noose hiding and dropping the noose over the heads of the birds. Ducks and other birds were cooked in an oven constructed by first strewing heated stones with wet grass. Birds were placed on the grass and covered with more grass, then more heated stones were put on top, and the whole lot was covered with earth. This way, the ducks were half-stewed.

Flora food included warrigal greens, muntries, and coastal Banksia cones soaked in water to extract the sweet nectar, which was then drunk, often mixed with wattle gum (called *jaaning* on the north coast of New South Wales). Also vanilla lily root, and salty, fleshy and glutinous pigface leaves, which, according to the explorer Edward Eyre, were eaten as 'a sort of relish with almost every kind of food'. It was a rich diet, consisting of over forty different fruits, berries, insects and resins.

On the plains and in the open forests people chose from a multitude of lilies, including the chocolate lily – the flowers smell of chocolate, but it's the tuber roots that are eaten; there's no chocolate taste. Other edible tubers included leopard, tiger and donkey orchids.

For thousands of years the Gunditjmara people of Western Victoria used the ingenious methods of channelling water flows to harvest fish and eels, then farming and smoking them. In this way they produced a year-round supply of food and goods to trade in one of Australia's first aquaculture ventures. This unique system of using the landscape carved by the lava flows for freshwater fishing is different to those mentioned in modern and historical records in other areas of Australia.

The Gunditjmara people developed this landscape by digging channels to bring water and young eels from Darlots Creek to low-lying areas. They created ponds and wetlands linked by channels containing weirs. Woven baskets were placed in the weirs to harvest mature eels. These engineered wetlands provided the economic basis for the development of a settled society with villages of stone huts, built using stones from the lava flow.

The five regions of New South Wales are the coastal tablelands, western slopes, western plains and highlands, with the climate on the coast being relatively mild, but half the western region prone to drought.

Some of the foods eaten there – in addition to animals and fish – were wattleseeds, the sugary gum and the sweet flower buds from the leopardwood; wild banana, which grows near mulga trees; and sarsaparilla bush leaves, which were chewed but also made into a drink sampled by Watkin Tench, first fleet diarist. Native cherry was (and still can be) eaten when the yellow fruit turns orange, and the roots of the native yam were eaten raw or cooked in hot ashes. The fruit of the sandpaper fig (*Ficus coronata*) could be eaten raw when ripe, and the leaves and flower stalks of the giant water lily were a treat. Geebung fruit were best when soft and left to ripen on the ground.

TASMANIA

It is generally conceded that the fate of the Tasmanian Aboriginal people, the Palawa – that is, their virtual extinction due to systematic slaughter and then disease – constituted genocide. From an estimated 3000 to 15 000 before colonisation, there are today few Indigenous Tasmanians left, and all of the Indigenous languages have been lost.

It is, then, difficult to build a picture of their food practices. And there is a lot of scholarly argument around their achievements. They were known to eat a lot of possum, kangaroo and wallaby, but it is believed they did not eat scaled fish. Pascoe provides evidence of abalone diving by Tasmanian women, abalone being a prized food, though not by the colonists, who called it 'mutton fish'. But then, as Pascoe points out, they boiled them whole, which gave them 'the texture of industrial rubber'. He records an Aboriginal recipe for poaching abalone in their shells on hot coals, which he tried, finding that 'it remained tender and even more flavourful.'

As for vegetable foods, in the absence of Indigenous names for foodstuffs, a short article by Liz McLeod and Bernard Lloyd in the magazine *Leatherwood* suggests that

> The [English] common names of many plants suggest
> their edibility: Native blueberry, carrot, sea parsley
> and sea celery, potato, cherry, and Native 'bread',
> apple berry, snowberry, kangaroo apple, and currant

bush, coffee berry, alpine raspberry, and also mint,
tea tree, sweet rush, pepperberry and so on.

There are records from early settlers. McLeod and
Lloyd quote from the diaries of George Augustus Rob-
inson, who spent time in Tasmania before becoming
the protector of Aborigines at Port Phillip in Victoria. He noted a fern called by the Bruny island locals
rully, and writes that 'the natives seemed filled with joy
when they met with a description of [a] fern tree called
rully, which is pleasant eating; this is far superior to the
other called *Lar*'. He also wrote of a fruit called by the
people *pur-rar*, and seeds 'like the french bean', called
poorner, 'which resembles a young shallot, and of which
the Bruny women appeared to be very fond'.

Capparis spinosa

Of course, many of the foods mentioned above would
not be palatable to western tastes. But many would.
For instance, the curiously named native pomegranate is actually an Australian version of the caper,
Capparis spinosa var. *nummularia*, and can be pickled and
used in the same way. Tim Low remarks that there are
another '17 or so native capers, all bearing fruits and all

apparently edible'. Wild gooseberries have a tangy cherry tomato taste; wild passionfruit, another *Capparis*, has passionfruit-flavoured pulp.

Of the animal foods (apart from kangaroo and emu), I have tasted only the magpie goose, which, had it been freely available, would be regarded as one of the most succulent game birds in the world. Happily, while this book was being edited, I learnt that it is finally about to be marketed. (See chapter 7, 'The producers'.)

Low's *Wild Food Plants of Australia* lists 180 plants. The definitive list of native foods, both flora and fauna – *Tables of Composition of Australian Native Foods* – lists over 500 items, admittedly enumerating different species of the same plant, but still an impressive number of foods that non-Aboriginal Australians have yet to sample. Yet even it is far from complete. One interesting example is the native truffle.

There are enormous numbers of native Australian truffles, very few of which have been sampled for taste and only a few – the desert truffle being the best known – eaten by Aborigines. Environmentally, the truffle is one part of a symbiotic triangle: the tree, the truffle and the animal that digs for and eats the truffle. The truffle grows on the roots of trees, protecting the root from soil-borne root pathogens. But the spores of the truffle are enclosed by an outer covering, and the only way they can escape and reproduce is by being eaten. Enter the smell. Truffles have powerful odours so that passing animals will root for them, eat them, then disperse the spores around the forest floor in their faeces. In Australia, these relations occur between native animals like the long-footed potoroo and the bettong and the eucalypts, casuarinas and paperbarks of the Australian bush.

There are far more species of truffles in Australia than in Europe, or elsewhere (I know of truffles in Africa and, and have eaten a Chinese truffle – not pleasant). There are at least 250 known species, with scientific speculation that there could be up to 1500. Will there be a Périgord truffle among them? So far, no one knows. A Victorian truffle expert, Dr Peter Stahle, has been quoted as saying that for gastronomic purposes, a truffle must have pleasing aroma, flavour and texture. Apparently, the native truffles so far tasted may have good aroma and flavour, but not the firm texture of the European truffles. In *Wild Food Plants of Australia*, Low mentions the desert truffle, *Elderia arenivaga*, and *Polyporus mylittae*, 'blackfellow's bread' among others eaten by Aboriginal people, without commenting on their flavour other than that 'Aborigines rated [blackfellow's bread] as a delicacy'. Chef George Biron tasted native bread, *Laccocephalum mylittae*, and was not impressed. 'It has the texture of a rubber ball, quite solid but slightly pliant, and I decided to bake it whole in foil to see if it had any flavour ... Bland is a bit of an understatement, but it least it was neutral, nothing unpleasant.' Only 1499 to go.

Surely among 1500 there must be one with a pleasing aroma, flavour and texture? It would be typical of

European Australians to discover a sensational native truffle, having spent so much time, effort and money in growing the European import. Australian native rice presents the opposite problem.

Native rice has been a part of the Indigenous diet in the north of Australia for thousands of years, although no one knows exactly how it was eaten. In a report on ABC Rural online in 2014 Lorraine Williams, a Larrakia woman working with Dr Penny Wurm (see below), says she wished she had thought to ask more questions of her elders as a child. 'I'm sad, because had I asked old people 20 years ago about how to prepare wild rice, we may have had more answers.'

There are four native species, all members of the genius *Oryza*, the same as conventional rices like jasmine and basmati. According to Dr Daniel Waters of Southern Cross Plant Science, Australian native rice can grow in a wide range of environments and because it has been geographically isolated from the cultivated rices, it contains more genetic diversity, which makes it a valuable resource. But don't hold your chopsticks waiting for a bowl. Dr Penny Wurm from Charles Darwin University has been researching native rice for over 20 years. The problem with the rice is milling. Conventional milling machinery won't completely de-husk the grains and some are broken in the process. 'That's the phase we need to get rid of,' said Dr Wurm. The research continues. If only it had begun long ago.

Again, had we started earlier, we could be eating

bread made from weeping grass, a perennial grass that could potentially produce more grain with more nutrition than wheat. Only now is the research being carried out. How many other native grasses could have been developed – grasses that are naturally drought-resistant and adapted to the land?

There is one more aspect of the Australian native foods discussion that needs to be addressed: the quite extraordinary level of nutrients in the foods growing in the 7 690 000 square kilometres of this continent, which stretches from just north of the Antarctic to just south of the equator, lapped by the Pacific, Indian and Great Southern Oceans. It doesn't have vast amounts of the rich deep soils of Europe – 20 per cent of Australia's land mass is classified as desert – rainfall is low, erratic (and getting more so), and climate zones, apart from the desert, range from tropical rainforest to temperate forests and a small area of snow-covered mountains. It is that variability and that difficult climate which contribute towards the nutritional density of native Australian foods. Why are these foods so rich in nutrients? Because they're wild; because they have to struggle to survive.

And as we have discovered recently, because the native foods are wild foods, they are all six to twenty times higher in antioxidants, anti-inflammatories, vitamin C, enzyme regulators, even mineral content and nutritional density.

It is strange that, knowing this, knowing that the

world is clamouring for these foods, knowing how they could improve the diets of both Indigenous and European Australians, there is no powerful financial support, either from government or private enterprise, to develop the production of and research into these foods. Apart from anything else, they are a unique national resource.

MAGGIE BEER

....

KANGAROO CARPACCIO WITH PERSIMMON, LIME, MOUNTAIN PEPPER AND EXTRA VIRGIN OLIVE OIL

Serves 6

The one native food I've used a lot is kangaroo. After Cheong Liew, I think I was the first to use it, back in the '80s. The Pheasant Farm restaurant I had then was a game restaurant, so it was the perfect food, and the international visitors just loved it. We had very sophisticated diners.

I did also use quandongs, but in those days they weren't very easy to get, and I never used fresh quandongs – they weren't available. Someone did send me some in the post once. Now with Outback Pride you can get fresh frozen quandongs – in fact, I used them in a dinner in London last September.

I think there's a new era coming, a new appreciation for Australian native foods. It's about time! This recipe is a play on two dishes that I did in London for Restaurant Australia.

72 g fresh kangaroo strip loin fillet, thinly sliced
    (note: three slices per serve = 12 g)
2 tsp mountain pepper, coarsely ground
1 persimmon, peeled and finely diced
6 segments lime
extra virgin olive oil, to serve
sea salt, to season

1. Ensure that the kangaroo strip loin is really well chilled, then thinly slice into portions approximately 2 mm thick, across the grain of the loin.
2. Place each portion onto a piece of cling film, then repeat this process, stacking the portions on top of each other. Return them to the fridge until ready to serve.
3. To serve, place the slices of kangaroo into the serving plate, then sprinkle over the mountain pepper and top with the persimmon, dividing it between the six servings. Place a segment of lime on each. Just before serving, drizzle with olive oil and season with sea salt.

Maggie Beer is one of Australia's best-loved cooks.

TONY BILSON

....

KANGAROO MERGUEZ WITH OYSTERS

*I think it's great that we're beginning to use these
ingredients. What's happening is we don't want to imitate
an old culture, we're in the stage of creating a new culture,
and that takes a long time.*

400 g kangaroo
400 g pork belly
400 g breast of mutton
20 g fine sea salt
4 g black pepper
4 g cayenne
8 g mild chilli powder
8 g pureed garlic
8 g pureed ginger
8 g ground cumin
8 g ground anise seed
10 ml olive oil
finely grated zest of one orange and one lime
8 thin sausage skins, soaked in ice water
Sydney rock oysters
lime

1. Cut the meat into 3 cm cubes and chill until firm.
2. Put the salt, pepper, cayenne, chilli powder, garlic,
    ginger, cumin and anise in a bowl and add just enough

cold water to cover them. Mix to a paste. Add more water if they begin to dry out.

3. Grind the chilled meat in a 4–6 mm (¼ inch) mincer. Mix the seasonings, oil and zest into the meat, keeping the mixture cold.
4. Fill the sausage skins and tie them at 6 cm lengths.
5. Grill or barbecue the sausages until cooked.
5. Just before serving, open the oysters, chill in salted iced water and plate. Serve three oysters and two sausages per portion, with a piece of lime.

Tony Bilson has been described as the Godfather of Modern Australian Cuisine. He has owned and cooked at many restaurants, and is today a consultant.

2

HOME-GROWN MARVELS

Terminalia ferdinandiana

But Jesus said unto them, A prophet is not without honour, but in his own country, and among his own kin, and in his own house.

Mark 6:4

It was around five years ago I began to read stories about the 'miraculous' noni juice from noni fruit. It was, we were told, from the morinda tree, native to Polynesia – especially Hawaii – and it was, we were told, miraculous stuff. Marketed as a cure for cancer, diabetes, heart disease, high blood pressure, arthritis, psoriasis, allergies, sinus infections, ulcers, menstrual cramps, depression, fatigue, chronic pain and much more.

It fulfilled all the criteria for a superfood. Little known, from a faraway or at least glamorous place and containing a secret ingredient, in this instance, xeronine. It even had its own guru, Ralph Heinicke, Ph.D. According to Heinicke, xeronine is an unrecognised essential nutrient that makes the immune system work better, though exactly how is unknown. It also allegedly makes our cells absorb more nutrients by binding to specific protein receptors (which are not identified). References to xeronine in literature, other than on a website promoting noni juice, are few.

At the time I mentioned this fruit from the morinda tree to a chef friend who used a lot of native Australian ingredients. 'You mean cheese fruit?' he said, 'I use it in desserts.' This sent me to *Wild Food Plants of Australia*, and there it was on page 40, great morinda fruits from the *Morinda citrifolia*, a.k.a. cheese fruit. Low writes: 'Great morinda fruits produce one of the most disgusting smells in the Australian bush, comparable to rotting fruit. The fruit is nonetheless edible, with flavour combining camembert cheese and custard apple. The mushy pulp is a good source of vitamin C.' Anyone eaten durian?

In *Tables of Composition of Australian Aboriginal Foods*, four samples of cheese fruit were analysed and found to be not all that rich in nutrients (though the number of nutrients listed in the tables is admittedly limited). According to Brand-Miller et al., one sample contained 56 milligrams of vitamin C. Compare that to the Kakadu plum, which was recorded as having a staggering 3152 milligrams in one sample.

What is interesting about this story is that in order to be hailed as a 'superfood' – which it is not – cheese fruit had to appear to come from somewhere else. As all of our daily food does. In 2009 the *Sydney Morning Herald* published a list of 'Top 10 superfoods.' They were:

» acai – 'this exotic berry from the Amazon'
» yogurt
» broccoli – 'loaded with vitamin C'
» lentils
» sweet potatoes
» blueberries – the blueberry is high in all sorts of good things including antioxidants, and is the basis for comparison with other foods: the 'blueberry standard'
» wild salmon – not even available in Australia
» goji berries – 'the most nutritionally dense food on earth'
» kale
» barley.

Let's go back to that blueberry standard. In a 2009 study conducted by the Rural Industries Research and Development Corporation (RIRDC), published as *Health Benefits of Australian Native Foods: An Evaluation of Health-Enhancing Compounds*, one group of foods 'exhibited superior antioxidant capacity as compared to the Blueberry standard'.

Native Australian foods. The foods that have been growing here for thousands of years, that we've virtually ignored for the 200-plus years we've been here. And if those imports are superfoods, ours are super-duper foods.

I apologise in advance to the careful scientists with whom I have been discussing this topic for the use of the term 'superfood', which annoys them intensely. But in this book, I am trying to communicate quite complex science to non-scientists, and that means to myself. Shorthand is needed. These are not superfoods or 'miracle' foods, and will not act as medicine to cure you of disease. They are just extraordinarily high in the compounds we need for our health.

Just one of the foods studied – the Kakadu plum – has been identified as being the richest source of antioxidant compounds in nature, and containing exceptionally high levels of vitamin C – 900 times higher than the blueberry standard in several samples – as well as vitamin E, folate and lutein. (Luteins are yellow to orange pigments found mostly in plants, and are related to vitamin A. Lutein is concentrated in the retina, so is necessary for normal vision, and is an antioxidant.) The Kakadu plum is also a good source of minerals required for genome health.

'We seem to think oranges are a good source of vitamin C,' said native foods supplier and scientist

Vic Cherikoff (about whom we'll learn more), 'but an orange is about 0.1 per cent vitamin C. You're looking at 50 times that in the Kakadu plum.'

Dr Izabela Konczak, the lead author of that RIRDC report, is from Poland, and came to Australia in 1999 to work on a project for CSIRO. When it was finished, she proposed a study of native edible fruits, herbs and spices. Said Dr Konczak:

> For me it was something. Vic Cherikoff presented me with my first sample of native Australian foods, riberries collected here in Sydney in a park. So it was very obvious that those fruits are readily available to anyone. I didn't know anything about them and that was an absolutely fascinating discovery. Later I found riberries growing in front of our building of the CSIRO.

The report that Dr Konczak and her colleagues produced found that (among many other things):

> All of the evaluated plant species were found to contain vitamin E and folate. Rich sources of lutein, a compound essential for eye health, are also present, as were magnesium, zinc and calcium, all important for the synthesis and self-repair of human DNA. Additionally, sources of valuable selenium were identified.

Selenium is an essential trace mineral, and is important for cognitive function, a healthy immune system and fertility for both men and women.

So how can you find these wonderful foods? Well, unless you live in a remote region where many of them grow, or can eat at a restaurant where they are served, for many of those we have just looked at, not easily. Some are becoming more readily available: my local greengrocer stocks finger limes, and you can find riberries growing on street plantings of lilly pilly trees.

But for Kakadu plums, Davidson plums and many of the less popular fruits, you'll need help. At the end of this book are two useful sections. One is the Appendix, 'A list of Australian edible plants, animals and grains', which, as the name implies, lists the most popular of these foods, including game birds and animals. The other is 'Useful contacts', a list of contacts for suppliers. We live in hope that more and more of our native foods will become easily available.

In recent years, both CSIRO and RIRDC have conducted research into the nutrient content of Australian native food plants. The more research that's conducted, the more it's confirmed that they are rich in the nutrients we need for health.

And it's not just the number of nutrients, it's the number of plants. The introduction to a report entitled 'Native Australian fruits – a novel source of antioxidants for food' (see the Bibliography, page 257) tells us that 'The number of fruiting rainforest edible plants in northeastern Australia (Queensland) has been reported to exceed 2400.' Now, while recognising that not all are edible – fruit can be toxic – this is still an extraordinary number of fruiting plants, many with equally extraordinary levels of nutrients. Is there a simple reason why this is so? In attempting to find out, I began with Gondwanaland.

Gondwanaland is the name given to the southern-most of the two continents – the other being Laurasia – that were part of a supercontinent called Pangaea which existed from (approximately, obviously) 500 to 200 million years ago. Around 200 million years ago, it separated from Laurasia and drifted further south. It consisted of today's Antarctica, South America, Africa, Madagascar and Australia, as well as the Arabian Peninsula and the Indian Subcontinent, which later moved north. There they were, all stuck together, crawling across the southern and creeping into the northern hemispheres.

The concept of Gondwana has been a very useful tool in freeing us from European paradigms, especially the ice age, which academic and writer on the Australian environment George Seddon reminds us 'looms large both in explaining current plant distribution and as a great renovator of soils, neither applicable in Australia'.

The convergence of many disciplines – ecology, genetics and ecophysiology, to name a few – which allows us to study the botany of the time has only emerged in the last thirty years, with new studies being published almost daily, so we're still learning. But what we do know is that, as gastronomic writer Deb Newell put it in her article 'A fork in the road', Gondwanaland meant 'millions of years of melee as Australia's offerings mixed it with that of the Malay Archipelago, a huge melange of animals and fruits and spices and greens – a little bit of old time with the fresh flavours of the new' – something like what appears on our restaurant plates today.

The result is that Australia is home to a large variety of unique and distinct flora not found elsewhere in the world.

The next two influences are climate and soil. Soil first.

Spread over almost 7 770 000 square kilometres, with one third in the tropics, Australian soils lie beneath our feet under climatic conditions from alpine to the Mediterranean zones of the south and southwest, to the wet and dry tropics of Queensland, to the very low rainfall areas of the centre, and have developed on a wide variety of rock types. Overall, Australian soils are ancient and are generally low in fertility and organic matter. This makes life difficult for today's farmers and gardeners. It also made life difficult for the flora that grew here, which, in the long run, proved a good thing.

But it was climate that provided the most profound influence. Australia is the world's second-driest continent – after Antarctica – with an average mean annual rainfall below 600 millimetres over 80 per cent of the continent, and below 300 millimetres over 50 per cent, at time of writing. The average January temperature over most of the country exceeds 30 degrees Celsius, but overnight frosts are common inland and it gets cold in the south. What has this got to do with plant nutrients? In a word: stress.

With such extremes of climate, plants need to protect themselves. 'Plants are stressed a lot,' said Dr Konczak. 'The elevated level of compounds in the plants help plant cells to survive. Also, soil conditions and the whole microclimate environmental factors would contribute.'

One food plant combines both Gondwanan and climatic influences.

Tasmannia lanceolata is the tree that produces the Tasmanian pepperberry and leaf. Dr Konczak says 'It is a very aromatic native pepper which was developed under the Antarctic climate' when Australia was attached to Gondwanaland. 'It had to protect itself from the cold and so developed a huge number of very different types of chemicals.' How many? The leaf alone contains alpha-pinene, sabinene, beta-pinene, p-cymene, limonene, beta-phellandrene, 1,8-cineole, terpinolene, linalool, alpha-terpineol, piperitone, alpha-cubebene, eugenol, alpha-copaene, methyl eugenol, alpha gurjunene, caryophyllene, aromadendrene, germacrene-D, bicyclo-germacrene, calamenene, cadina-1,4-diene, elemol, palustrol, spathulenol, guaiol, 220 MW sesquiterpene,

218 MW sesquiterpene 1, drimenol, polygodial and unidentified volatiles (from the Australian Native Food Industry Limited website, www.anfil.org.au).

Back to the question. Why does this country have so many fruiting rainforest plants – angiosperms, the ones that flower like gum trees and wattles – and why do their fruits have such high levels of nutrients? There is no simple, clear-cut reason for such a complex development.

I asked Dr Maurizio Rossetto, the principal research scientist and manager of Evolutionary Ecology at the National Herbarium of New South Wales in Sydney. He replied, 'We are actually doing some interesting work asking that same question as we speak.' He went on to say, 'Obviously, like everything in science, there is no short answer to it and there are many factors contributing to that outcome, some relating to phylogeny, some to selective pressures, some to chance.' (Phylogeny is the evolutionary history of an organism.) But he did have a stab, saying, 'Well, a simple interpretation that is emerging from our work is that dispersal is one of the main factors impacting on the distribution and assembly of rainforest plants.'

In other words, the expansion/contraction events that rainforest vegetation went through during geological times is likely to have favoured species that produce easy-to-disperse fruits. Easy to disperse in the sense that they are eaten by animals, then their seeds excreted. These include a lot of fleshy-fruited species.

While this is not the whole answer, as Dr Rossetto said, 'It goes some way to explain this pattern.'

I'll leave the last words in this ongoing search for origins to George Seddon: 'So the character of Australian flora is the outcome of many forces. Gondwanan origins played a part, but continental isolation, increasing aridity and various historical contingencies have also led to major modifications ... The story has no end.'

Finally, on the subject of 'miracle' foods, check your dictionary. My online dictionary just told me that a miracle is 'an extraordinary and welcome event that is not explicable by natural or scientific laws and is therefore attributed to a divine agency'. In other words, Jesus turning wine into water. Not necessarily noni juice.

But these foods – miracle or not – and more, as outlined in the previous chapter, formed the diet of the Aboriginal inhabitants of this land. Until Europeans arrived and trampled all over the Indigenous diet. The consequences of that change are only too well-known.

ANDREW FIELKE

....

OYSTER AND LEEK TARTLET WITH FINGER LIME 'CAVIAR' BEURRE BLANC

Serves 4

juice of 2 lemons (80 ml)

150 g diced cold unsalted butter

sea salt

1–2 tsp sugar

3 or 4 finger limes

2 medium-sized young leeks, washed and trimmed

oil for deep frying

50 g butter

white pepper from the mill

16 oysters

4 x 60 mm (approx.) sour cream (preferably) or
   shortcrust pastry tart shells, pre-baked blind (these can
   be bought frozen at most supermarkets)

5–10 g salmon roe

1. To make the beurre blanc, reduce the lemon juice in a
   stainless steel saucepan to about a third of its original
   volume. Swirl in the butter cubes a few at a time, until
   it is all incorporated. Keep warm. Do not allow to boil.
   Season to taste with the sea salt, and balance the acid
   with a little sugar.

2. Cut the finger limes in half crosswise and squeeze out the flesh, removing the seeds, if any. This is the 'finger lime caviar'.

3. Cut a 60 mm long piece of the pale section of each leek, and slice lengthwise into fine julienne. Heat the oil to 150°C and deep-fry the leek julienne until *light* golden brown and crisp. Remove and drain, and store in a bowl lined with absorbent paper in a warm place.

4. Slice the remaining leek into fine rings and simmer in 25 g of the butter *gently* until tender. Season to taste with the white pepper.

5. Warm the oysters *gently* in the remaining 25 g butter – do not overcook. Stir the finger lime caviar into the beurre blanc.

6. Place some warm stewed leek into each tartlet, followed by 4 warm oysters each. Top the tartlets with the beurre blanc and the crisp leek. Garnish with salmon roe.

Andrew Fielke is a Consulting/Guest Chef and native food distributor. His website is tuckeroo.com.au.

MATT STONE

....

KANGAROO LOIN WITH AUSTRALIAN NATIVE FRUITS, HERBS AND SPICES

Serves 4

Kangaroo is in my opinion the most sustainable meat we can be eating in Australia. It only eats wild food, not modified feeds. It's extremely lean and full of nutrients. I think we should be eating a lot more of it.

The roo is best served rare. Taking it out of the fridge some time before cooking will ensure it cooks evenly. I use this method for all red meats that I'm grilling. I love to cook meats on a wood-fired grill or barbecue, but if this is not an option, a hot pan will do the job.

When preparing the quandongs, be sure to keep the seeds. Inside them is a small nut that has a beautiful marzipan flavour and is great to infuse into milk or cream for a sauce or ice-cream base. If you're not going to use them within a week or so, place them in the freezer and they'll keep for months. The native fruits bring a very acidic flavour to the dish to cut the gaminess of the roo and the richness of the sauce.

The 7 spice is a very fragrant spice mix. The ingredients can vary due to season, availability and personal taste. If you like it hot, double the amount of mountain pepper. This spice mix is perfect on barbecue meats, vegetables and fried bugs. If possible, get fresh herbs like lemon and aniseed myrtle and dry them yourself. Whole pepperberries, wattleseed and bush tomatoes are commonly available. Note that this recipe uses dried and ground spices.

Set yourself up well for this dish and it will all happen very quickly.

600 g kangaroo tenderloin
250 ml beef broth jus
6 quandongs
50 g riberries
50 g desert lime
4 rosella flowers
50 g muntries
2 tsp 7 spice
400 g warrigal greens
2 tsp butter
1 cup mixed beach herbs (salt bush, barilla, beach
    mustard, beach banana)

Aussie 7 spice
1 tsp bush tomato
1 tsp lemon myrtle
1 tsp wattleseed
1 tsp pepper leaf
1½ tsp mountain pepperberry
½ tsp aniseed myrtle
1 tsp mangrove myrtle

1. Prepare the 7 spice ahead of time by simply mixing all the ingredients and storing in an airtight container or jar.

2. Kangaroo fillets will often be very clean when you buy them from the butcher. If there's any visible sinew, trim it away with a sharp knife. Place the roo loins in a bowl and add 1 tsp of the 7 spice and 1 tsp salt. Mix well and leave on the bench until the meat comes up to room temperature – about an hour. If using a fire or barbecue, be sure to light it well in advance so there is plenty of time to get a nice even heat.

3. Make sure your native fruits (quandongs, riberries, desert lime, rosella flowers and muntries) are defrosted. Run a small knife around the quandong and the seed should come out easily. Tear the rosella flowers into petals. Leave the other fruits whole.

4. Pick all the warrigal leaves from the stems and wash well. Pick and wash all the beach herbs. They're great fresh, but if you're using the salt bush, try frying it. This will give a crisp texture and bring out a lovely green olive flavour. Simply heat about 200 ml of vegetable oil to a high heat and carefully place the picked salt bush leaves in. Stir and cook for 2 minutes then quickly drain through a sieve and place onto some kitchen paper to dry. (The oil can be used a few times to fry any herbs, so strain it well and keep in the pantry.)

5. Place the beef broth in a smallish pan, leaving enough room to fit all the fruits in. Place on a medium heat and bring to a simmer. Add the fruits and leave to gently simmer.

6. Place the roo on a hot barbecue. Leave to caramelise for about 4 minutes, then turn. Cook for a further 4 minutes, depending on the thickness of the loins. (I really encourage you to cook the roo to rare. If that's not to your liking, medium is OK, but if you're heading to well done town, it will get very dry and chewy.)

7. Take the roo off the heat and leave to rest for the same amount of time you cooked it for.

8. While the roo is resting, heat a large pan and throw in the butter and a small splash of oil. Once the butter is melted and bubbling, add the warrigal greens. Cook for 3 to 5 minutes, stirring often, until the greens are wilted.

9. When the greens are almost done, throw the roo back onto the heat to warm again. By this stage, the fruits should be nice and soft. If the sauce has reduced too much, add a splash of water to loosen it up.

10. Drain the greens of any extra liquid. To drain them really well, you can place them on a tea towel and squeeze them. This will also help to keep them warm while you carve the roo.

Matt Stone is a chef who cares deeply about soil, farming, sustainability and Australia. He has collaborated with sustainable restaurateur Joost Bakker for a number of years. At twenty-one, he took on Neil Perry in the inaugural *Iron Chef* television show, and lost by four points.

3

A DISASTROUS CHANGE OF DIET

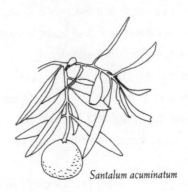

Santalum acuminatum

The typical diet came to consist of white flour for
damper, white sugar for tea, camp pie, salt and
beer, a combination we will recognise as the classic
nutritional disaster of industrialization.

Michael Symons, One Continuous Picnic:
A Gastronomic History of Australia

There's a knock on your front door. You open it. There's
a stranger there, pleasant enough; says he's looking
around the neighbourhood for somewhere to live. You
invite him in, give him a cup of tea. He goes on his
way.

Some time later, he appears at the door again. This time with several friends, some of whom you really don't like the look of. Somewhat reticently, you invite them in. Gradually, they begin to take over your house. You thought they only wanted to look around, but it becomes obvious they're not going away.

They bring in their own food, spread themselves around all the rooms, trash your furniture, clog up your plumbing and generally wreck your house, while hardly taking any notice of you. Eventually you find yourself sleeping in the backyard. They've taken over completely. You might call them the uninvited guests.

This is, more or less, what happened in what we now call Australia when the first Europeans arrived, although as an allegory it doesn't begin to describe the impact and the devastation that European invasion visited on the Indigenous inhabitants and the land that they had turned, over millennia, into what Gammage has called 'the biggest estate on earth'.

In his book of that name, Gammage writes, 'Aboriginal landscape awareness is rightly seen as drenched in religious sensibility, but equally the Dreaming is saturated with environmental consciousness. Theology and ecology are fused.' You've probably heard of totems. Before 1788, each individual had a totem. This totem carried a multitude of responsibilities, primary among them to ensure the survival of that totem. Gammage writes of one man he met whose totem was the maggot, a most important link in the chain of creation.

The longest war fought by Aborigines against the European settlers was on the Hawkesbury. In 1788, the Dharug people received Governor Phillip hospitably when he surveyed the river. Then, in the 1790s, he instructed farms to be built there. *Dharug* means yam, and the yam was a major totem. The Europeans who stole the land where the Dharug used to farm and cultivate yams – for the original inhabitants did farm and cultivate – took land, yam, totem and trade (the Dharug traded their yams with adjoining groups). Gammage writes, 'The clans fought back for 22 years, until all were dead or in hiding.' The yams were more than food, they were 'totem allies needing help'. Europeans did not understand this.

If you watched the first episode of the ABC adaptation of Kate Grenville's *The Secret River*, you might remember the scene where the Aboriginal visitors to the Thornhill land become angry at his digging up of a little daisy to plant a cereal crop. That was a yam daisy.

A totem is more than a badge. Aboriginal theology is complex, but a totem, as Gammage explains, is 'a life force stemming from and part of a creator ancestor'. So to a man or woman whose totem is the emu, they are emus. They must care for the emu and its habitat.

The complexity of relations between food and spirit can be seen in this story also told by Gammage. On Bathurst Island in the Northern Territory, when women harvest yams they always leave the top and cover it with earth. While understanding that this will grow more yams, they explain it by saying that if they dig it all out, then the food spirit will get angry and won't allow any more yams to grow in that place. Theology and ecology are fused. We can see, then, that taking Aboriginal land involved a lot more than forcing a devastating change of diet on Indigenous Australians: it was the destruction of a culture.

But not only did European Australians ignore the foods that grew here, they actively discouraged the hunting and collecting of traditional food. The authorities considered such practices primitive and undisciplined, and believed they had no place in the process of 'advancing' Aboriginal society. 'Advancing', in this sense of the word, meant 'assimilating' – a strange policy, that, in the words of Tim Rowse in his book *White Flour, White Power: From Rations to Citizenship in Central Australia*, 'both wooed and compelled, invited and manipulated'.

It was no more clearly explained than by Paul (later Sir Paul) Hasluck when he was Minister for Territories in the Menzies government, a post he held from 1951 to 1963. In that post he was most certainly one of the architects of assimilation, which he saw as 'The object of native welfare measures. This means in practical terms, that in the course of time, it is expected that all those persons of Aboriginal blood or mixed blood will live like white Australians do.'

The desired end point of assimilation was an obedient, trouser- or skirt-wearing, hardworking Australian citizen, albeit of darker hue. What part did diet play in this process? The answer is 'rationing': handouts of flour, tea, sugar, tobacco and occasionally meat to the local Indigenous people.

'From the 1890s,' writes Rowse, 'rationing began to replace violence as a mode of government.' The massacres could not be allowed to continue, because they seemed to be having no effect on the behaviour of the Indigenous people, often simply making them more belligerent. So both missionaries and pastoralists came to the conclusion that rationing was 'a way of rendering cross-cultural relationships peaceful and predictable'. Soon, the administration saw the light and rationing became official policy. In 1928, the Chief Protector of Aboriginals in Queensland 'urged the government to standardise rationing according to consistent principles' which would 'enhance [Aborigines'] value as machines'. You can see where this assimilation business was heading.

In most cases, of course, there was no need to corral the people into a rationing depot. Firstly, the spread of settlement, with the land covered by huge flocks of sheep and cattle, made the traditional way of life more and more difficult. And secondly, as anthropologist Annette Hamilton pointed out in the mid-60s, 'The twin principles which kept the Aboriginal society functioning were the need to find food and the desire to limit effort in doing so.' A vital element in a hunting and gathering economy is to preserve the energy input/output balance favourable to human survival. 'When the news came that the whites had abundant, if strange, food, more than they could possibly eat, this was like news ... of the super water-hole.'

And just as they had always moved to the source of food, they moved to the white men and their settlements, not to take part in white society, not to experience social change, but to eat their food.

At first the rations were given to supplement native foods. Then, as settlement increasingly denied Aboriginal people access to food and water, they began to develop tastes for beef, flour, sugar, tea and tobacco, and, as Hamilton writes, 'the comfort of a blanket, the luxury of soap'. But in many outback areas, the official rations were inferior in quality and insufficient in quantity. They were just sufficient to encourage Aborigines to stay near the ration depot, but not enough to give them one square meal a day.

As the widely admired anthropologist W. E. H. Stanner wrote in 1938:

Most of the detribalised and semi-civilised natives would be shown [by experts making a tour of Australia] to be badly under-nourished ... Many of them are short of essential proteins, fats, minerals salts and vitamins. The number of Aborigines just over the threshold of scurvy, beri-beri and other deficiency diseases must be very great.

The cultural results of this attempt at assimilation by diet can be seen to this day. But they were obvious back then to those who looked closely. A Melbourne writer, R. H. Croll, wrote of an Aboriginal man he met at Hermannsburg in the 1930s who, because he was dependent on the white man's supplies, and no longer had the skill to hunt meat 'could no longer live as a blackfellow'. Of course, it was more than the loss of hunting ability. At the time, very few Europeans understood the connection between country and spirituality. One, biologist H. H. Finlayson, observer of the Luritja and Pitjantjatjara people, came close in 1933 when he wrote of 'the miserable wreckage of the race which is strewn about the margins of the settlement; for nothing is more striking than the swift demoralisation and degeneration which follow the renunciation of his own way of life for dependence on whites.'

How little European Australians understood that relationship between country and culture – and health – can be seen in this excerpt from a 1944 book, *Citizenship for the Aborigines* by A. P. Elkin, an English-born clergyman and anthropologist who studied Aboriginal life and religion, yet could still write: 'The absence of villages and gardening is a difficulty which … can be overcome.' Needless to add, it wasn't.

But what is most surprising is the tenacity of Aboriginal people's understanding of the relationship between food, environment and spiritual life, even after 160 years of determined attempts to 'wean' them from their traditional foods.

The writers of a report published in 2013, 'Factors influencing food choice in an Australian Aboriginal community', spent three years in a remote community recording interviews with people on their current food choices and their knowledge of traditional food choices. Sixteen people (eight men, eight women) within an approximate age range of 35 to 60 years were selected for interview.

Firstly, the researchers observed that the older participants in the study 'demonstrated deep and intricate knowledge that underpinned daily food choice'. That knowledge extended to the influence on harvesting a particular food crop of the winds, tide, lunar cycle, star formations and the flowering of plant species. All had been learnt, over time, through story, song, dance and experience. They also learnt that 'Strict laws also governed food procurement, preparation, and distribution' and the consequences of disobeying those laws. Remember, these interviews were conducted in 2013, at least 160 years after Europeans had actively suppressed Indigenous food culture.

Not surprisingly, based upon their deep understanding of their own foods, they at first believed that European Australians with whom they came in contact had a similarly comprehensive understanding of their own food system. They assumed that the knowledge related to such things as food origin, preparation method and seasonal availability enabled non-Aboriginal people to live in balance with their food environment and so, like them, make informed food choices.

But when they were confronted with having to 'gather' European food – from shops – they had no point of reference:

> [Our] foods, we go by season, what [food] is good for that season. Like [food] from the shop we don't go by season, we only walk in and buy what things we want. We get them, but sometimes we don't know, for picking up meat, or chicken. We don't know which date that chicken got killed and supplied to the shop, we don't look at the month, which month – yes – some non-Aboriginal people they are clever, they walk in and get [food] and they look at the dates, [and] buy. Us, sometimes we don't – never grew up on that system, we just walk in, we get them, what we want, and then go buy 'em.

This report refers to others cited by anthropologists and ethnographers on the ways in which in Indigenous culture food was integrated into all aspects of life, providing links to country. Taken together, these papers give a picture of a complex system where foods chosen gave people a sense of time, place, identity and responsibility; food was a central tool and theme in teaching and knowledge acquisition, and played a major role in society and ceremony. And, as we will see, a food plant can have multiple uses, as medicine, fibre, etc.

Interestingly, the report found that during the mission era – from the 1940s to the 1960s – there was a sense of balance for these people because their traditional foods augmented the inadequate rations that were handed out. One respondent said, of that time:

> There were two different kinds of food at the same time; it was like a balanced diet kind of foods, one from the [traditional] side and the other from the [introduced] side, that's how we lived on. They were afraid of the whitefellas, afraid of what to eat … When they first tasted it, it was like they were only testing it, what kind of food the whitefellas ate, but some felt that that food did suit them. From then on the people ate two different kinds of food, it was food that the whitefellas introduced and also our natural foods. They wanted to go on eating these foods … just to be sure that the traditional foods are always here for us.

Another said:

> He [mission superintendent] would give us enough. Just a handful of everything and that was it. What was given we ate, and went, and we didn't come back to get more. We went away and collected wild honey and all those natural foods. Maybe we have forgotten all the bush potatoes, yams, and so on … We only had a little bit, and little bit for each day.

But as the interviews went on, the older people noted that the new foods, which they called 'the new-comers', were taking over, and making up a larger and larger part of their diet. They began to associate these newcomers with other signs of deterioration in their lives: social issues such as low employment, low school attendance, gambling, substance abuse. Not to mention the physical problems of diabetes and obesity. Their lives, they said, were 'out of balance'. And they began to learn the ways in which Europeans assess their foods: 'The non-Aboriginal people they say, there's too much sugar in this one, this is healthy food, this food will make you grow big and fat, this one has plenty of iron. They talk about protein, energy, saturated fat, sugars, carbohydrates, sodium, and potassium.'

And their awareness transformed into anxiety about the younger generation:

> They reckon I am only telling them lie story. I always talk to my kids, have *gapu* [water] all the time, it is good for your body ... Even we tell them – because it is already advertised on TV [television] – that Coke is no good or even Sprite or Fanta or Solo, stuff like that. It is already there, they're already watching it on TV. That is why they go in and buy stuff like that.

The young, they worried, had lost the knowledge of the traditional food system which they felt was a base upon which to build an understanding of food generally. They no longer had any control: 'Don't know what's happening in factory [where food is produced] – sweat, might not wash hands, or allergic when eat, see symptoms – eating something not good for them … Our system from long time ago, only eat fresh one – changes happening.'

Now, of course, 'fresh one' is expensive. Money has replaced hunting and gathering skills. A young participant told the interviewer that the 'fruit and vegetable group is missing' because on a limited budget, these foods were 'too risky'. The fusion of theology and ecology had been replaced by nutrition and economy. The more money you had, the better you ate. The Indigenous skills of hunting, gathering and farming the land had no currency. European Australians had imposed their own agriculture.

LAKLAK BURARRWANGA AND FAMILY

HOW TO KILL AND COOK A TURTLE YOLNU STYLE

In the book Welcome to My Country, *there is a narrative recipe for killing and cooking a* miyapunu *(turtle) that I found intriguing for a couple of reasons. Firstly, the use of the shell of the turtle as an oven. And secondly, the use of a leaf from the djilka tree (the grey bark tree, Drypetes deplanchei) as a herb to add flavour. I have also included the method of killing the turtle, as it vividly illustrates the Yolnu connection to their food source. It does not come from a supermarket on a polystyrene tray covered in plastic. JN*

» First we prepare the *miyapunu* for cooking. Djawa kills the *miyapunu*. He hits it over the head with a rock or an axe to stun it. Then he puts a sharp stick in the head through the brain to kill it. He cuts its head off and pulls the guts out through the neck. He draws out the liver, the intestines, all sweet and fatty. This female *miyapunu* has *mapu* in her, soft ones, and we pull them out to cook. We don't have a pot here so we will cook the *mapu* (eggs) on the sand by covering them with ashes. We have built up a big fire for the *miyapunu*, so there is a lot of hot sand we can use to cook the *mapu*.

» We dig through the hot sand and bury the *mapu* taken from inside the *miyapunu* together with the *mapu* collected on the beach. Maybe ten minutes later they're ready. The *mapu* are salty and rich. They taste like the sea. We might also eat the first of the *miyapunu*, the inside parts, at the same time. Nothing is wasted. That's respect.

» To start cooking the *miyapunu*, we put stones in the fire to heat them up. We stand the *miyapunu* on its back legs and put the stones inside the shell with some *djilka* leaves, the ones used for the smoking ceremony, as herbs. The *djilka* have got a really good smell. They'll make the meat good and tasty. You put those leaves in with the stones and wait half an hour or so. We get a soup from that mixture, a salty, fragrant broth that comes from the inside of the shell where the meat had been soaked through with the herbs. We'll all take a drink of that soup – old people, young people, all of us. It's good. It makes you feel strong and alive.

» Now we put the *miyapunu* in the fire to cook. We put some ashes on the top too and wait about an hour until it is ready. It's softer to cut now. We cool it down with sea water.

Laklak Burarrwanga is an Elder of the Datiwuy people, a caretaker for the Gumatj clan and an Honorary Associate of the Department of Environment and Geography at Macquarie University. This recipe is from Laklak Burarrwanga and family, *Welcome to My Country*, Allen & Unwin, Sydney, 2013, pp 29–30.

4

THEY BROUGHT THEIR OWN

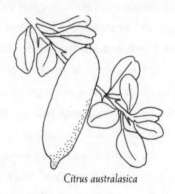

Citrus australasica

They must certainly be furnished at landing with
a full year's allowance of victuals ... with all kinds
of tools for labouring the earth ... with seeds of
all kinds of European corn and pulse and garden
seeds ... and after that ... they might undoubtedly
maintain themselves without any assistance
from England.

Joseph Banks

It was on 12 November 1787 that the ships which
would become known as the First Fleet, consisting of
eleven ships, weighed anchor in the Cape of Good
Hope and set sail for the country that would become

Australia. According to Watkin Tench, a lieutenant in the marines on board, the fleet carried, in total, 987 officers and men, marines and convicts, most of whom were men, with some women and children. One of the soldiers, a marine, died on the voyage, as did twenty-four convicts. They landed at Botany Bay on 18 January 1788, having set out from Portsmouth on 13 May 1787. After less than a week at Botany Bay, they decided it was unsuitable, and moved up the coast to Port Jackson, where, it had been ascertained, there was a better supply of water.

They were to begin a colony in a land that had not been properly explored beforehand. Cook and his crew had merely made landfall on the east coast, stopped at Botany Bay for a few days and sailed up the coast. No subsequent voyages were sent to reconnoitre. They had come halfway around the world to an unknown land, but they didn't come empty-handed. Along with 'trinkets for the natives' they arrived not only with their own food but with their own methods of agriculture from the other side of the planet – methods that would prove disastrous, not only to the land but to the 50 000 years of culture and cultivation of that land. But they had been warned, by Cook, on the basis of scant evidence, that 'there was hardly anything fit to eat' in their new land.

Largely ignoring what grew here, the occupiers planted and raised what they had brought with them. Crops of wheat, barley and maize, European fruit and vegetables were planted and imported livestock herded, first by the colonial government with convict labour and then by emancipated convicts and free settlers, utilising European agricultural methods on a land ill-suited to it. And what grew, flew, walked or ran along the ground here was largely ignored, unless it was familiar to the new settlers, the exceptions being readily recognisable fish, molluscs and game birds.

While it made perfect sense for those journeying to an unknown land to bring their own food, it did not make sense to almost entirely turn their backs on what was growing and eaten here, or how the Indigenous people cared for and cultivated the land.

Let me take a detour to tell the story of one of those exceptional foods. Tetragon, known today as warrigal greens or New Zealand spinach, was noted, collected and eaten by Cook and Joseph Banks in 1770. On May 6, Cook wrote, 'We dined today upon the stingray and his tripe ... We had with it a dish of the leaves of tetragonia cornuta boild, which eat as well as spinage or very near it.' It was eaten by the crew of the *Endeavour* to allay scurvy, and seeds were taken by Banks, along with many others, to Kew Gardens, where it was successfully propagated. Banks, the Swedish botanist Daniel Solander and the Finnish botanist Dr Herman Spöring, also on the voyage, collected a large amount of Australian flora, around 800 specimens of which were illustrated in the *Banks Florilegium*. (Here it is worth remembering

Cook's note that 'there was hardly anything fit to eat.')

Tetragon certainly made an impression on Banks, perhaps because of the point of reference with a European food plant: spinach. By 1788, Banks had become a general adviser to the English government on Australian matters, and in that capacity wrote a report to the government to help in the planning of the First Fleet to the new colony.

He wrote there were 'some' edible vegetables, 'particularly a Sort of Wild Spinage'. From Kew, tetragon found its way to France, where it was naturalised. The story is now taken up by pioneer native produce chef Jean-Paul Bruneteau, who, on a visit to the south of France, twenty-three years after he had left there as a twelve year old to come to Australia with his parents, found something in his uncle's garden:

> In 1989 … I went to France. When we arrived at my uncle's place [in the south] he had a beautiful garden with everything growing. And there in the corner was a patch of warrigal greens. I said, 'Where the hell did you get these from?' And he said he'd been growing it for ages, 'It's tetragon,' my uncle said. 'You used to eat this stuff when you were a kid.'

In a later conversation with me, Bruneteau said, of his interest in native produce: 'I just did what any Frenchman would do in a new place. I looked around for something to eat.' Unlike the first settlers.

As if to prove that the composition of the fleet was hardly conducive to, or designed for, the business of settling in a new and foreign land, a colony that would need to be fed, there were, on board, only one professional gardener (who was only twenty years old) and one fisherman. But this did not deter Governor Phillip from getting started. In February, he selected a site at Farm Cove and put Henry Dodd, his valet, who had worked on Phillip's estate in Hampshire as an agricultural labourer, in charge of setting up the first garden. Dodd had much to contend with, including the poor quality of the Sydney soil, the difficulty of clearing the bush, and the much commented on sheer laziness and ignorance of the convict labourers.

At first sight, the heavily wooded shores of Port Jackson had looked promising for agriculture. On closer inspection, the soils were found to be sandy, shallow and, as they learnt, lacking the nutrients for planting what they had brought with them. From England they had brought carrots, potatoes, lettuce, asparagus, onions, broccoli, beans, peas, watercress, wheat, barley, rye and oats. Also apples, pears, plums, cherries and a selection of citrus, including navels, Seville oranges and Tahitian limes.

In Rio de Janeiro they had picked up tamarind, prickly pear plants, complete with, and specifically for, the cochineal grubs (the first but not the last botanical blunder – the pear later ran rife and became an environmental problem), coffee, cotton, lemon, orange and guava.

And in Capetown, they added rice, maize (then known as Indian corn), apples, bamboo (the second environmental error), pears, strawberries, quinces, apples, an assortment of trees and 500 head of assorted livestock, which included a bull, a bull calf, and seven cows. (One of the cows died at sea.) Also aboard were four goats, twenty-eight pigs and forty-four sheep – for mutton, not wool – only twenty-nine of which survived the year. Only the goats prospered, climbing in numbers from nineteen on 1 May 1788 to 522 registered in 1794.

While there were plenty of tools, they were of very poor quality. Barbara Cameron-Smith, author of *Starting from Scratch: Australia's First Farm*, writes 'to Governor Phillip's obvious disgust, the cheap tools fell to pieces.'

In that first planting, very little of the wheat survived, and most of the barley and other seeds rotted in the ground. Most of the fruit varieties they brought with them from England didn't survive without a cold winter to set the fruit. The soft fruits were eaten by native insects. Citrus fruits and figs did better, but needed fertiliser to grow well in the nutrient-poor local soil.

They didn't entirely ignore what grew locally. Tench believed that a drink made from native sarsaparilla (*Smilax glyciphilla*) saved many from scurvy. And he wrote: 'A few wild fruits are sometimes procured, among which is the small purple apple mentioned by Cook, and a fruit which has the appearance of a grape, though in taste more like a green gooseberry, being excessively sour. Probably were it meliorated by cultivation, it would become more palatable.' This last astute observation – that cultivation would render native produce more palatable to European tastes – was virtually ignored, sadly, until the 20th century, when chefs like Raymond Kersh and Andrew Fielke worked very hard for many years, with little success, to interest Australians in their own produce.

Notwithstanding smilax and experiments with native fruit, not everything the colonists tasted was successful. As Cameron-Smith writes: 'A group of marines suffered the consequences of eating too many ripe fruit from the rusty fig, *Ficus rubiginosa'*. But they did find edible plants like wild celery (*Apium australe*) and samphire (*Sarcocornia quinqueflora*), shot ducks, netted fish and discovered the Sydney rock oyster.

But it was not long before illness set in. On 25 March 1788, Cameron-Smith quotes Surgeon Smyth reporting that there 'are now upwards of 200 sick in the hospital on shore', suffering in the main from 'true camp dysentery and scurvy'. The imported cattle escaped almost immediately and made their way up the Nepean River some 40 miles (64 kilometres) beyond Parramatta, where they prospered, and were found in 1795.

Disputes over food with the locals began early. Tench reported that 'When fish are scarce, which frequently happens, they often watch the hauling of our seine, and have more than once been known to plunder its contents.' The scarcity was because of the extra strain put on the fishery by the huge increase in population. The balance had been upset. In the circumstances Tench noted sternly, 'The only resort ... is to show a musket.'

After the dismal failure of the crops at Farm Cove, Phillip came to the conclusion that free settlers with good tools and a knowledge of farming were essential and he wrote to the British government requesting them. He also sent boats to Batavia and India for supplies, but by February 1790, the storehouse had only enough food for four months. By May 1790, starvation appeared imminent. Tench wrote: 'Three or four instances of persons who perished from want have been related to me.'

The Second Fleet arrived on 3 June 1790, and replenished the stores, but also brought around 1000 additional mouths to feed. Drought didn't help. In November 1790, Phillip wrote: 'I do not think all the showers of the last four months put together would make twenty four hours' rain.' Leaving behind the nutrient-poor soils of Sydney, in November 1788 Phillip established public farms, using convict labour, at Rose Hill (today's Parramatta).

They clear-felled the land and planted wheat and maize and stocked cattle, horses and sheep at Emu Plains, where 'they surprised everyone by making a profit.' Phillip also developed plans to allot land to convicts whose sentences had expired for their own farms. By the end of November, James Ruse, Australia's first white farmer, was allowed to occupy and cultivate 30 acres of land at Parramatta. Ruse reaped his first crop in 1790. A year later David Burton, the Public Gardener, listed 918 acres of land in Parramatta either cultivated or cleared. By the time Phillip left in 1792, there were sixty-eight small farms around Sydney.

As these plantings and stockholdings increased and prospered there was, understandably, pride in the achievement of transplanting European farming methods and crops to this distant land. Colonial historian Grace Karskens quotes Lorraine Stacker, writing much later of an enormous field of wheat on the Emu plains: 'turn the eye which way you will, you have the most delightful and almost boundless prospect' – a glimpse into the future of broadacre (monocultural) farming.

But the transformation of the land to grow more European food inevitably led to degradation. The activity that Karskens notes in 1804 in the Castle Hill area, where 'six hundred convicts were continually employed in felling trees to open roads through the forest', would be repeated across the entire country for at least the next 150 years. Curiously, the clear-felling of the trees was not in and of itself necessarily a bad thing. But it was an example of the ways in which these first settlers arrived on a continent which already had a complex land management plan in place, and trampled over it with their heavy boots. Clear-felling facilitated the overstocking of their imported animals, compacting the soil and encouraging run-off rather than allowing the rain to soak into the soil.

Before 1788, as Gammage writes, 'Soft soil let water soak in rather than run off, so less rain sustained more plants.' He quotes James Cotton, a Cobar (New South Wales) pioneer:

> before this district was stocked ... [it] was covered with a heavy growth of natural grasses ... The ground was soft, spongy and very absorbent ... a gradual deterioration of the country used by stock ... has transformed the land from its original soft, spongy, absorbent nature to a hard, clayey, smooth surface ... which instead of absorbing the rain runs it off in a sheet as fast as it falls.

The by-product of this change in soil was that rivers, once gentle, became roaring torrents because the water was not absorbed. This fast-running water scoured gullies, causing erosion. In such ways was the landscape changed by its new inhabitants. The pride in their achievements came before the fall of the environment.

As New South Wales reached the twentieth year of European settlement, a farming settlement was beginning to establish itself in Tasmania. In 1801, John Oxley, then a visitor to the new colony, wrote of the state of settler farms at New Town Bay, 'White cottages in the midst of tolerable good gardens afford a pleasing contrast to the wilderness of the surrounding scenery', but the reality was that few of these settlers 'understood anything about agriculture; they have in consequence so exhausted the ground by repeated crops of the same grain that it produces little or nothing.'

Appearances were more important than reality, and by 1825 a visitor to Tasmania wrote that the estates of the wealthy settlers (described by Michael Symons in *One Continuous Picnic* as 'near-feudal') offered vistas of 'nature subdued by art' and the gardens, with their English flowers, 'looked and smelt like home'. This idea of wilderness being outside the fence is something that was alien to the pre-1788 stewards/farmers of the land. Gammage writes: 'Australia had no fences in 1788. Some places were managed more closely than others, but none were beyond the pale.' The gulf between European and Indigenous farming methods was, and remains, insurmountable.

In 1864, Edward Abbott, author of the first Australian cookbook, *The English and Australian Cookery Book*, was inspired to write a poem entitled 'A Tasmanian Picnic', describing a spread that would not have been out of place in Warwickshire or on the banks of the Cam:

For there was a store of viands good –
Beef, mutton, lamb and veal;
And tongues, and lambs, and suckling pigs;
As fat as e'er did squeal … .

And puddings crammed so full of plums
The cook 'was sure they'd bust!'

Just three years before the publication of Abbott's poem, on 25 February, the Acclimatisation Society of Victoria – the first of a number of such organisations – was formally established at a public meeting presided over by His Excellency Sir Henry Barkly, then governor of Victoria. The Acclimatisation Societies were evidence of the belief of the time that nature was a series of building blocks that could be taken apart and put together again. For centuries, Europeans had been moving plants around their half of the world with no noticeable deleterious effects – even the forced migration of plants and animals of the Columbian Exchange had caused little damage and much enrichment of cuisines. But none of these movements had encountered a land so different in its ecology – not a word much understood in the 19th century – as Australia.

In their desire to re-create the environment, the diet and the recreations of the land they had left, and having decided, as the Acclimatisation Society of Victoria had, 'that none of the native plants was worthy of cultivation, that the native animals neither provided decent game nor were worthy of domestication, and that the native birds sang nowhere nearly as sweetly as those back home', they set about stocking the land with all that they missed.

From rabbits and foxes to hunt, to trout and carp

to fish, privet and bamboo for their gardens and camphor laurels to provide shade, every single one of these introductions – perhaps with the exception of the trout – caused serious environmental problems. Of these introduced problems, the worst, perhaps, was the rabbit. 'After many attempts,' as Thomas Dunlap writes in his essay 'Remaking the land: the acclimatization movement and Anglo ideas of nature', 'the settlers succeeded in establishing European rabbits in Australia. That was in the early 1860s. In 1887 an Intercolonial Royal Commission offered a reward of £25,000 for something to get rid of the animals.' To this day, carp infest our rivers and threaten our native fish, and foxes decimate native as well as introduced fauna. All efforts to rid the land of rabbits have failed, and there have been many. Two rabbit-proof fences were established, one in Queensland in 1893, and one in Western Australia in 1907: unfortunately, rabbits can jump and burrow. In 1950, myxoma virus was released, causing the population to drop from an estimated 600 million, but by 1991 genetic resistance set in and the population climbed again to 200–300 million. Starting in 1991, a new biological weapon, calicivirus, was released, with some success. But we still have rabbits.

Other serious environmental problems persist as a result of European farming practices.

The Murray–Darling Basin covers much of inland south-eastern Australia and consists of 11 000 kilometres of waterways – the fourth-largest river system in the world. It is the nation's most important agricultural region, producing one third of the nation's output – mainly wheat cropping, grazing of sheep and cattle, and intensive irrigated horticulture – for an annual production of $10 billion. This level of intensive production has taken a severe toll on the environment because the economic development of the basin has required the clearing of native vegetation, the damming of rivers, the heavy irrigation of vast tracts of the semi-arid inland (areas that for millennia received an average annual rainfall of less than 25 centimetres) and the introduction of destructive foreign plants and animals.

Today, the soils in the basin are nutrient-deficient (as they already were in New Town, Tasmania, in 1804), thin and easily flood-damaged; increasing acidity and rising salty water tables are severe problems. The evidence is abundant: the relentless desire to impose an alien food culture and agricultural regime on the continent has left it dangerously depleted.

Rather than attempt to understand their methods of caring for the land, the first settlers treated the original inhabitants as nothing other than native fauna, as expressed in an editorial in the *Sydney Morning Herald* in 1838:

> This vast land was to them [Aborigines] a common
> – they bestowed no labour upon the land, their
> right, was nothing more than that of the Emu or the
> Kangaroo ... The British people ... took possession

... and they had a perfect right to do so, under the
Divine authority, by which man is commanded to go
forth and people, and till the land.

Not all early settlers saw it that way. Gammage
quotes Edward Curr, pioneer squatter on the Murray,
who observed: 'It may perhaps be doubted whether any
section of the human race has ever exercised a greater
influence on the physical condition of any large portion of the globe than the wandering savages of Australia.' (Curr wrote this in 1883; his use of the phrase
'wandering savages' was ironical in intent.)

Evidence of the intense and intricate Indigenous
land management was there for all to see – and it
was seen by many Europeans. In the 1820s, Robert
Dawson wrote: 'It is impossible ... to pass through
such a country without being reminded of a gentleman's park and grounds.' ('Park', at the time, meant the
carefully attended grounds surrounding a gentleman's
estate 'at home'. The use of the word 'park' to mean a
public space was not current in 1788.) Dawson was not
the only European to make such an observation. Gammage quotes John Oxley noting that south of Walcha
in north-western New South Wales he found 'the finest
open country, or rather park imaginable: the general
quality of the soil excellent.'

But the parks have gone. Overgrazing had a trans-
forming effect. Of our bushfires – Black Thursday on
6 February 1851 and Black Saturday on 7 February

2009 – Gammage wrote: '[they] are not controlled and lit to manage the landscape' but out of control and 'devastate and decimate species which flourished during millennia of Aboriginal burning'. (Controlled burning, as practised before 1788, is again being used to restore the land with the savannah enrichment program – see chapter 7, 'The producers'.)

As Gammage points out, there is no way to return to 1788. The Australian population is too massive, too urban, too dependent on monoculture, herbicides, pesticides and petrochemical fertilisers.

And perhaps it was too much to expect of the Georgian colonists that they would take notice of the 'wandering savages', let alone ask them how they cared for country and what they ate to remain so healthy. It has taken the colonisers more than 220 years to learn that, as Gammage has written of the Indigenous people, 'Land care was the purpose of life.' How different might have been our land and our food culture if European Australians had taken notice of the Aboriginal people rather than doing as they did: pretending the original inhabitants weren't here.

Of course, not all shunned native produce; there were experiments and exceptions. But, ultimately, the new arrivals turned their backs on it.

SIMON BRYANT

....

WARRIGAL GREENS AND DESERT LIME PESTO WITH WHOLEMEAL PASTA

Serves 4

A little practice cooking with native Australian ingredients will bring great rewards. This recipe features a few harder-to-get ingredients, but I say get used to eating them – they're the future! The beauty of the native ingredients in this dish is that they stand up to the robust wholemeal pasta, which can sometimes overpower pasta sauces with its earthiness.

Warrigal greens are a leafy vegetable similar to spinach. As an alternative, good old English spinach would suffice. Some caution should be used with warrigal greens, as the leaves contain toxic oxalic acid (also found in rhubarb leaves), which can be harmful for some people if consumed in large quantities. To remove the oxalic acid, it's a good idea to blanch the leaves first.

Sea parsley is a bit like parsley on steroids. (You can substitute dark-green, hardy flat-leaf parsley, but you will need to use double the quantity.) Desert limes are punchier and sourer than regular Tahitians, so my substitute would be a small preserved lemon. These native limes freeze really well, so grab a bunch if you see them. (They also make the greatest addition to vodka and tonic, so they won't go to waste.)

I seem unable to kill my warrigal greens and sea parsley, no matter how much love I don't give them. The seedlings are available from good nurseries, but if you just want to buy some to try, get Googling.

250 g warrigal greens, leaves picked, baby leaves
    reserved, to garnish
1 large handful sea parsley leaves and stalks, roughly
    chopped, a few leaves reserved, to garnish
juice of 3 lemons
250 ml (1 cup) extra virgin olive oil, plus extra to cover
200 g macadamias
about 30 desert limes, plus a few halved limes, to garnish
4 cloves garlic, peeled
salt flakes and cracked black pepper
60 g (3/4 cup) grated parmesan
500 g wholemeal or spelt pasta
extra virgin olive oil, for drizzling
cracked black pepper and salt flakes
shaved parmesan, to serve

1. To make the pesto, first blanch the warrigal greens in a
    large saucepan of boiling water for 1 minute, then rinse
    them in cold water. Drain well and squeeze out excess
    liquid.
2. Roughly chop the blanched greens and the sea parsley
    and place them in a food processor with the lemon
    juice and a little olive oil. Blend until the greens are
    roughly pureed. Add the macadamias, limes and garlic

and continue to blend until the mixture looks like crunchy peanut butter.

3. Continue blending slowly while drizzling in the remaining olive oil until you have a coarse pesto, then season to taste with salt and pepper. Add the parmesan and pulse to blend through, then check the seasoning.

4. Transfer the pesto to sterilised jars. Let it settle to remove any air bubbles, then cover with olive oil. This makes about 750 g of pesto. Store it in the fridge for up to 3 months. If you want to eat the pesto as a dip, add a little more oil to thin it down.

5. Cook the pasta in boiling salted water until al dente, then toss it in a little olive oil to prevent it from clumping together. Fold in 100 g of pesto per serve, drizzle with olive oil and season with black pepper.

6. Make a salad of the reserved warrigal green baby leaves, sea parsley and desert limes. Season with salt to taste, then add a little olive oil and pepper.

7. Divide the pasta among bowls and garnish with the salad. Serve with shaved parmesan and a small bowl of extra pesto to the side, if you like.

Simon Bryant worked in The Grange kitchen in the Hilton with Cheong Liew, was the co-host with Maggie Beer of ABC TV show *The Cook and the Chef*, and with Paul Henry ran the last Tasting Australia event in 2014. This recipe is from *Simon Bryant's Vegies*, published by Lantern (Penguin Australia), 2012.

5

FROM BANDICOOT CURRY
TO VEGEMITE

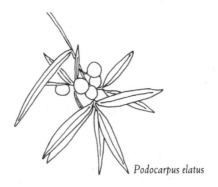

Podocarpus elatus

Famine was now approaching with gigantic strides.

Watkin Tench, November 1789

On 7 July 1864, the *Argus*, a Melbourne morning news-paper (1848–1957) ran a long report on page four of the second annual dinner of the Acclimatisation Society of Victoria. This society, you will recall from the last chapter, was formed to import into Australia from the Old Country flora, fauna and fish that were not available in the new one. But this worked both ways.

The society also exported Australian foods and plants deemed worthy of being added to the menus and landscape of Britain. One such being Murray cod, a freshwater fish much admired by the colonists. Perhaps the purpose of this dinner was to discover more native foodstuffs worthy of export. According to the *Argus*, it was:

> To discover what, within the limits of the colony, was eatable – to range the kingdom of Nature in search of meat – to test the esculent capacity of many of God's creatures as could possibly be brought within the art of cookery – this was the wider and more daring aim of the diners last night.

The menu, entirely in French – as was the custom for large, important dinners of the time – both in language and for course names (*Le Gibier* for the game course and *Entremets* for the sweet course, for example) – contained some daring dishes. For example, *'Le fricandeau de wombat aux epinards'* (thinly sliced wombat served with spinach), *'Le bandicoot en currie'* and *'Le pate chaud de perroquets'* (warm pâté of parrot). In addition, there were dishes of kangaroo, black duck, magpie goose (which I have already written about), Murray cod and other Indigenous fare. All in all, it was well-received, some dishes more than others:

> If among our beasts, we have nothing better to offer than a bandicoot or a kangaroo, we have among our birds the bustard or wild turkey which need not fear

competition with anything that flies. The black duck and the magpie goose are also worthy in their kind to rank with the best of imported birds.

It's worth noting, but not unexpected, that the only member of the vegetable kingdom on the menu was *'Les yams de Queensland'*. And even then we can't be sure that they were native. Even less welcome than kangaroo and bandicoot on the early Australian table were the fruits, vegetables and herbs of the land.

The nameless journalist summed up by proclaiming that 'The novelties, approved by the eye and the tongue, require only labour and patience to become a familiar possession, and a part of the wealth of every man in the colony.' As we know, this didn't happen.

Perhaps we shouldn't be too hard on the First Fleeters for turning their backs on the local food. They – convicts and soldiers – had been through a lot. To begin, with, having spent thirty-six weeks at sea, the vast majority having never been to sea before, they'd arrived in an alien land about which they knew nothing. And as they moved out from the environs of Port Jackson into 'the bush', and began to farm the land, look around, and take it all in, they saw a place where, as one settler writing home put it:

The appearance of light green meadows lured squatters into swamp where their sheep contracted rot; trees retained their leaves and shed their bark instead, the swans were black, the eagles white, the bees were stingless, some mammals had pockets, others laid eggs, it was warmest on the hills and coolest in the valleys, [and] even the blackberries were red.

The landscape was not only alien, but forbidding. It had 'The wild appearance of land entirely untouched by cultivation', as described in *The Voyage of Governor Phillip to Botany Bay*. That description could also have done for the locals. The encounters with the Gadigal, naked human beings carrying spears and boomerangs, whose language and customs were totally incomprehensible to the colonists, were equally frightening for both parties. *The Creek of the Four Graves* by Charles Harpur (1813–68), the son of convicts and described as the first native-born Australian poet of any consequence, is a long epic poem which tells the story of five settlers whose trip to the interior turns to tragedy when they are attacked and murdered by a group of Aborigines. But even before this, they are aware 'Of danger lurking in its forest lairs'. When the tribesmen attack, and one of the five flees, and fires on them:

His deadly foes went thronging on his track.
Fast! for in full pursuit behind him yelled
Men whose wild speech no word for mercy hath.

The Indigenous people are depicted elsewhere in the poem as nothing more than 'painted savages', whose right to the land is not at issue. Nor could he have known that their language contained 'no word for mercy' .

Is it any wonder that the colonists wanted nothing to do with the food of these scary people? Indeed, would famously starve waiting for provisions from the Old Country rather than eat the food of the other – the wild, untamed, uncivilised, naked other.

Food, as we know, is far more than a material substance which is ingested and excreted. It distinguishes and defines us to ourselves and to our fellows. It can be a primary cultural marker of our clan, tribe, religion, region, province, personal sensibilities and country.

Fast forward to today's Australia and Australians and there's one food that could well be the best predictor of national identity of any food in the world: Vegemite. If you eat Vegemite, if you like the black, salty, sticky, sharp-tasting industrial spread, you are almost certainly Australian. Until globalisation, travelling Australians would either take jars with them or have them sent in care packages. In Tunis, the capital of Tunisia, I met the vicar of the only Anglican church in that city. He was Australian, and he invited me for a cup of tea – with toast and vegemite. Vietnamese people feel the same deep connection to pho, Ethiopians to their spongy bread, injera, northern Italians to their polenta, southerners to their pasta. And just as the first Anglo-Celts to settle in Australia stuck rigidly to the foods of their origin, so too did the migrants who arrived from the 1950s on, bringing with them, as did the First Fleeters, their ingredients.

Native produce was not entirely ignored by the new arrivals, but their use of it was opportunistic or surrounded by cultural hedges. I have already noted Watkin Tench's belief that a drink made from native sarsaparilla saved many from scurvy. The problem of scurvy prompted Philip to make the most of available fresh foods, and in a despatch he mentioned 'wild celery, spinages, samphose, a small wild fig, and several berries which proved most wholesome'.

And beyond the merely medicinal, native foods were used for all manner of reasons, including survival and even feasting (of game meats). There was, in the early days, a whiff of adventure around their consumption, to do with hunting and exploring, being out in the wild. But, as Bannerman writes in his article 'Indigenous food and cookery books: redefining Aboriginal cuisine', they also 'represented failure: the depletion of stores, extreme poverty, or separation from the society of "home" and were seen as second best.'

Settler Katherine Kirkland harvested the tubers of the yam daisy or maranong (elsewhere here murnong) and wrote: 'I have often eaten maranong; it is very good; and I have put it in soup for want of better vegetables, before we had a garden.' Conversely, some settlers actually enjoyed native food plants. In northern Queensland, cookbook writer Mrs Rawson said of bush yams that they were 'not unlike sweet potatoes when unearthed, but have a far nicer flavour, more nutty'.

Sometimes it's hard to understand the attitudes to local produce, without invoking that cultural hedge. Louisa Ann (Mrs Charles) Meredith wrote in her book Notes and Sketches in New South Wales during a Residence in that Colony from 1839 to 1844 that the snapper was:

very nice though not esteemed a proper dish for a dinner party why I am at a loss to guess; but I never saw any native fish at a Sydney dinner-table – the preserved or cured cod and salmon from England being served instead, at a considerable expense and, to my taste, it is not comparable with the cheap fresh fish.

Even when serving the food of the land, the hedges were built. In 1846, the governor of New South Wales, Lieutenant-General Sir Maurice O'Connell, held a banquet at which was served kangaroo, wallaby and wonga pigeon. Visiting soldier Godfrey Mundy wrote of the framing of the banquet that: 'the general appliances of the household, the dress of the guests and the servants, were as entirely English as they could have been in London', while the ingredients of the dishes on the menu were a long way from British.

There was wallaby tail soup, boiled 'schnapper' with oyster sauce, a haunch of kangaroo venison and wonga pigeon with bread sauce. The surprising inclusion of so many local foods in one menu was either an early and self-conscious attempt at nationalism or, more likely, a culinary entertainment. A bit of a lark.

The first Australian cookbook, written in Tasmania in 1864, was *The English and Australian Cookery Book*. Its frontispiece proclaimed it to be 'For the Many, as Well as For the "Upper Ten Thousand"', and it was written by 'An Australian Aristologist' (aristology is the art and science of cooking and dining), later revealed to be one Edward Abbott, a grazier and founder of the *Hobart Town Advertiser*, whose family had arrived in 1790; in other words, one of the 'upper ten thousand'.

In many ways this curious book set the tone for many Australian cookbooks to come, although, in the fashion of the time (and especially in the manner of Mrs Beeton), it was as much an instruction book for its dedicatees – 'His Fair Countrywomen of the "Beautiful Land"' – as a compilation of recipes. The recipes were mainly British, with a smattering of 'continental' – gazpacho, 'sour-krout', Turkish pilau – with a nod in the direction of his new home: roast 'emeu', roast wombat, and a selection of kangaroo recipes, including the famous Slippery Bob, kangaroo brain fritters. Food historian Colin Bannerman remarks that 'his recipes for kangaroo suggest it was widely accepted both as a survival food and as meat for the well-served table.' But such local delicacies are overshadowed by imports like Devonshire squab pie, jugged hare, Irish stew, Banbury cakes and, from the Raj, mulligatawny soup.

To give Abbott his due, he does offer a comprehensive list of Australian game and fish. His record of fish is especially interesting as it catalogues fish and seafood from New South Wales, Victoria, South Australia and Tasmania.

But it was his kangaroo recipes that are the most quoted, even today. You'll find a modern day version of his kangaroo steamer by food historian Jacqui Newling in this book (see page 99). He quotes, with obvious approval, from journalist, publisher and author Henry Melville's 1851 book *Present State of Australia, with Particular Hints to Emigrants*: 'the flesh of the kangaroo is, perhaps, the most nutritious and easily digested of any known to man.'

One striking feature of the book is the total absence of any native flora or any mention of Indigenous inhabitants. Even in the lengthy section on servants, it is assumed that they will all be European.

My copy of *The Commonsense Cookery Book* – undated, but judging by one of its advertisements for Waugh's Baking Powder featuring a Light Horseman (headline: 'Call to Waugh'), more than likely published between 1914 and 1916 – is remarkable for containing not one recipe that would identify its Australian origin. *The Schauer Australian Cookery Book*, my copy without front and back pages (circa 1946?) does contain one concession to place. After the recipe for 'Ox Tail Soup', there is an instruction that 'Kangaroo tail soup can be made in the same way.'

The Goulburn Cookery Book, first published in 1895, with no revision of the text for thirty years, was the work of Jean Rutledge (Mrs William Forster Rutledge), and written, as she said herself, for 'women in the bush who often have to teach inexperienced maids and would be glad of accurate recipe that anyone of fair intelligence could carry out.' My edition, the thirty-third, printed in 1928, contains not a single recipe using Australian produce.

As the population moved to the cities, separated from the hardships of the bush and even minimal contact with the Aboriginal population, interest in and use of native foods gradually declined. In the first edition of the Country Women's Association's *Coronation Cookbook* in 1937, there was a chapter on emu eggs, offering six recipes using them: scrambled, boiled, in sandwiches, omelette, baked cheese savoury and pound cake. By the next edition, the emu eggs had disappeared.

Until very recently about the only item of native produce regularly used in Australian homes was the macadamia nut, a piece of produce that owes its popularity to being first farmed in Hawaii. In spite of being a food prized by Indigenous Australians for thousands of years, it was only 'discovered' by English botanist Alan Cunningham in 1828, named (after Australian scientist Dr John Macadam) in 1857 and first planted commercially near Lismore in 1882, two years after seeds were first sent to Hawaii. They flourished in the Hawaiian environment and the first macadamia processing plant

ever built began operating in Kakaako on the southern
shores of the island of Oahu: you need tough machinery to crack the tough shell.

Hawaiian they may have remained had it not been
for an upsurge of tax minimisation schemes involving
macadamia farms in the 1980s. But while a lot of ini-
tial investment started that way, the industry started
making a profit, farms became bigger and now it's a
strong and sustainable industry. The other advantage
the nut has is that it's not known as *gyndl* or *jindilli* or
boombera, some of the Indigenous names for it. Why do
I say this? Because now we are coming to what I believe
is the dark, underlying reason for the long rejection of
our native foods. But first, the not so dark.

Firstly, cultural determinism, which basically means
you stick with what you grew up with. That is why it
was only sensible that the First Fleet brought its own
food. Secondly, neophobia, the fear of the new, in this
case new foods. And new they were. Giant marsupi-
als that bounded across the landscape; a goose called
a magpie; limes shaped like fingers; flour – *nardoo* –
made from a fern. Large white tree grubs. Strange grub
indeed.

And thirdly, a concept of the French sociologist
Pierre Bourdieu, 'habitus' – another and more complex form of cultural determinism, defined by Loïc
Wacquant (another French sociologist and an associate of Bourdieu) as 'the way society becomes depos-
ited in persons in the form of lasting dispositions, or

trained capacities and structured propensities to think, feel and act in determinant ways, which then guide them'. In other words, the sum total of 'Englishness' or 'Frenchness' in an individual. When that individual changes countries, they bring with them a package of traits and habits that identify them with their origins. These traits are as disparate as gestures, ways of sitting, walking and, of course, eating.

I should add that habitus refers to more than just national traits. Wacquant wrote extensively of the 'pugilistic habitus' of the denizens of a boxing gym on the south side of Chicago. But here, we are interested only in the culinary habitus of the Anglo-Celt settlers of Australia. An example of the power of that habitus is the continuation, to the present day, of the ritual of a hot Christmas lunch or dinner in a land where Christmas is characterised by a searing sun and not freezing cold. Only now is that ritual being broken down.

But are these three enough, in combination or alone, to explain 220-plus years of a population ignoring the proposition that, as Waverley Root put it, 'food is a function of the soil, for which reason every country has the food naturally fit for it.' The food most of us still eat is the food we brought with us at different periods. Surely there must be another reason for such a long period of turning our backs.

Interviewing pioneer Australian native food restaurateur Jean-Paul Bruneteau, I asked him why we had never cultivated or hybridised some of these foods over the years, as was done with the tomato when it first went to Europe, for example. He responded:

> It drove me nuts asking that question. I think there's a couple of things. I've often described it as food racism. The English were here for a long time before anyone came to disturb them. And to them, anything the blacks touched was black food. For example, why is roo regarded as a pest or described as vermin when in actual fact it's one of the cleanest, healthiest, most beautiful meats? It was because the sheep farmers wanted it off their properties instead of it cohabiting [with the sheep], which they're doing now.

Food racism. Hard to prove, hard to pin down. But I can corroborate his reference to the kangaroo. Visiting a large sheep station near Nyngan, during the course of a conversation with the owner, a prosperous and highly intelligent man, apropos of what I can't remember, he began a violent rant about the 'filthy kangaroos' sharing the paddocks with his sheep. The law, until relatively recently, agreed. Kangaroo was only approved for human consumption in South Australia in 1980, and in all other states in 1993.

Was it food racism that saw the introduction of rationing? In chapter 4, I quoted Rowse writing in *White Flour, White Power* that 'rationing began to replace violence as a mode of government.' By violence, he meant the wholesale slaughter of the Indigenous people, replaced mainly because these massacres (amply documented by Henry Reynolds and others) weren't working: that is, rather than subduing the Aboriginal population, they increased their belligerence.

The other method of 'wiping out' the Aboriginal people was less violent; it was called assimilation. In 1867, the editor of the *Rockhampton Bulletin* – Queensland had been the site of some of the worst massacres – wrote against 'the ruthless and indiscriminate extermination of the doomed race' and went on to claim: 'Their extinction is only a matter of time, and no unnecessary cruelty should be used to effect a result which the operation of natural causes will certainly accomplish.'

The 'natural causes' he was speaking of were the various mechanisms of assimilation, a project which led to such practices as removing 'half-caste' Aboriginal children from their families and placing them with white families, or in government or church-run institutions, where they would 'learn to be white', creating the Stolen Generations.

During a 1937 conference of Commonwealth and state Aboriginal authorities, A. O. Neville, Chief Protector of Aborigines in Western Australia, said in a speech to his colleagues: 'Are we going to have a population of 1,000,000 blacks in the Commonwealth, or are we going to merge them into our white community and eventually forget there were any Aborigines in Australia?'

And to support this attempt at what Henry Reynolds is not afraid to call genocide, we recruited, admittedly inadvertently, white flour, sugar, tea and tobacco. But I can't help asking, if the aim of those such as Neville was to 'forget there were any Aborigines in Australia', and they had known the devastating results both spiritually and physically of cutting the Indigenous population off from their traditional food sources, would they not have redoubled their efforts?

Racism in Australia is a complex problem. Over sixty years of migration, Australia has absorbed a remarkable number of nationalities – the Sydney suburb of Bankstown alone contains upwards of 130 – with an enviably small amount of racial conflict. The riots at Cronulla, due to complex causes which I have written about elsewhere, were unique in Australian history, it is fair to say. Even the more recent disquiet with and among Islamic communities is not as disturbing as vested interests would have us believe.

It's not hard to find racism against Aboriginal people in Australia today. A 1997 study looked at 'Prejudice against Australian Aborigines: old-fashioned and modern forms'. Prejudice, I'd submit, is another word for racism. By old-fashioned, it meant the beliefs that

Whites are biologically superior to Blacks, and that the races should be segregated. The expression of racist sentiments is overt, obvious, and recognizable ... Old-fashioned racists prefer to segregate Blacks

in employment, schooling, housing, and the like,
and also believe and/or express strong negative racial
stereotypes such as 'Blacks are lazy, dumb, shiftless,
etc.'

Modern racism, on the other hand, is more cunning
and subtle, and has three elements:

First, the belief that Blacks are becoming too pushy,
they are not behaving like deprived minorities have
in the past, and they do not deserve their gains.
Unlike old-fashioned racism, it is believed that Blacks
have the right to opportunities, but that they want
more rights than everybody else. Second, people's
attitudes are not based on their own experience.
Finally, modern racism is expressed symbolically. For
example, affirmative action programmes are seen to
symbolize unfair demands ... modern racists believe
discrimination against Blacks does not exist any
more, that racism is bad, and that their views are not
racist because they are based on empirical facts.

The study found that 'while 57.9 per cent of
respondents scored above the midpoint on the
modern prejudice scale, only 21.2 per cent did so on
the old-fashioned scale.' The results suggest that the
modern form of prejudice against Aboriginal Australians is stronger and more pervasive than the old-
fashioned form, although a sizeable minority of the

sample did score high on the old-fashioned prejudice scale. The prevalence of both forms of anti-Aboriginal prejudice in this study indicates that prejudice is an endemic social problem.

The complexity of white Australia's prejudice against Aboriginal Australians was highlighted by the 2015 controversy surrounding the Indigenous Australian Rules (AFL) footballer Adam Goodes, who was booed by the crowd whenever he appeared. Online comment was heated, with many asserting that it was not racist, it was only a comment on his way of playing, or on the 'war dance' that he had performed during one game. It continued for many weeks and only abated when Goodes took a break from the game for a week.

But now we come to the good news. Bob Dylan was right. The times they are a'changin'. Yes, we are beginning to accept the foods that grow here. But in the 21st century, this brings a new set of problems.

JEAN-PAUL BRUNETEAU

....

ROLLED WATTLESEED PAVLOVA

When making meringues of any sort it is imperative that the whisking bowls and whisks are not greasy. It is also vital that no speck of egg yolk is present with the whites, as even a minute amount of yolk is enough to prevent the whites from stiffening. An oven at 150°C is the precise temperature for the perfect pavlova. More or less than this heat will dramatically alter the result.

Don't add too much of the mud, or it may curdle the cream. If you wish, you can use an emu egg. One emu egg is equivalent to 12 hen eggs, but there really is only enough to make one pavlova. The flavour isn't compromised.

50 g macadamia nuts, roasted and unsalted
100 g hazelnuts, roasted
100 g pecan nuts, roasted
115 g (½ cup) caster sugar
1 heaped tsp cinnamon
6 egg whites
1 tsp vinegar or strained lemon juice
335 g (1½ cups) caster sugar
200 ml cream
2 tbsp Gundabluey Mud (see recipe on page 98)

1. Preheat the oven to 150°C. To make the sugar crust, chop the macadamia nuts to large crumbs in a food

processor, and set aside. Repeat the process with the hazelnuts and pecans, and set aside. Place the 115 g of caster sugar and the cinnamon in the food processor and whizz for 15 seconds. Add all the set-aside nuts and whizz for a further 20 seconds.

2   Line an open-ended Swiss roll tray with greaseproof paper. Use a little water to fix the paper in position, on the underside of the paper only.

3. Whisk the egg whites with the vinegar or lemon juice until soft peaks form. Add half the 335 g caster sugar gradually to the whites, whisking until the whites are stiff. Fold in the remaining sugar.

4. Empty the entire contents of the mixing bowl onto the prepared tray in one clean sweep, using a rubber spatula. This helps keep air pockets to a minimum. Spread the mixture evenly, using a goose-neck spatula, if you have one.

5. Sprinkle the crust mixture evenly over the meringue. Bake in the oven at 150°C for 20–22 minutes. Remove the meringue from oven, place a clean tea towel or a large sheet of greaseproof paper over the top and invert it onto a cake rack. Allow to cool.

6. Trim the four sides of the pavlova with a serrated knife and carefully remove the greaseproof paper.

7. Whip the fresh cream until it starts to thicken. Add the Gundabluey mud and continue to whip until stiff.

....

GUNDABLUEY MUD

The mud is made through the absorption of water by the roasted ground wattleseeds over a very low flame. It is important never to boil the seeds, as the flavour becomes 'dusty' and bitter. The mud stores well in the refrigerator for up to a week if well covered with a plastic wrap seal.

110 g roasted and ground wattleseed
600 ml water
pinch salt

1. Cook the wattleseed with the water and salt in an open stainless steel frying pan to allow quick evaporation. Simmer, reducing the volume by two thirds, or until the grounds meet the surface of the liquid. Do not boil.
2. Blend the cooked grounds in a blender at high speed until they become a smooth mud.
3. Scrape the contents of the blender into a clean container, allow to cool and then seal. Store in the fridge until you need it.

Jean-Paul Bruneteau is a French–Australian chef, and a pioneer in the development of an authentic Australian cuisine. In his kitchen at Rowntrees, and then Riberries, native Australian foods were skilfully incorporated into a European context. This recipe is from Jean-Paul Bruneteau, 'Wattleseed recipes', in *Tukka: Real Australian Food*, HarperCollins, Sydney, 1996, pp. 200–211.

JACQUI NEWLING

....

KANGAROO STEAMER

Serves 8, with bread and condiments

The steamer is mentioned as a curiosity in various letters and journals from the 1820s, and recipes were eventually published in Australian cookery books – three are given in the first Australian-authored cookbook, The English and Australian Cookery Book: Cookery for the Many, As Well As for the Upper Ten Thousand, *published by Tasmanian politician Edward Abbott in 1864.*

This recipe works best when made over two or even three days, allowing time for the flavours to develop, before and after cooking. You will need a good-quality heatproof jar with an airtight lid, or a glass or earthenware pot sealed with a double layer of foil and string, the way you would seal a plum pudding.

500 g kangaroo fillet, coarsely minced or finely chopped
400 g speck (or pancetta), finely diced
1 onion, finely chopped
250 ml (1 cup) port wine (or fruity red wine)
2 tsp salt
½ tsp ground white pepper
½ tsp ground mace (or ground nutmeg)
½ tsp ground allspice
2 tbsp thyme leaves

1 bay leaf
3 juniper berries

1. Put all the ingredients except the bay leaves and juniper berries into a large, non-metallic bowl. Using your hands, mix the ingredients to form a slightly sticky but sloppy mixture. Refrigerate for a few hours, or overnight.
2. Pack the mixture into a clean 1 litre jar to just below the fill line, as the mixture will expand during cooking. Use a table knife to remove any obvious air pockets and place the bay leaf and juniper berries on the top. Seal the jar firmly.
3. Put a trivet in the bottom of a large saucepan or stockpot. This allows water to pass beneath the jar and minimises the risk of it cracking from exposure to direct heat. Place the jar on top of the trivet. Fill the pan with enough cold water to reach three quarters of the way up the sides of the jar. Bring the water to the boil, reduce the heat and simmer for 3 hours, topping up the water as necessary to keep the jar immersed to the three quarters level.
4. For safety reasons, allow the water to cool a little before removing the jar from the pan – take care, as the jar will be wet and slippery.
5. Refrigerate and serve cold, as you would rillettes or a terrine.

From bandicoot curry to Vegemite

Jacqui is the resident gastronomer at Sydney Living Museums. This recipe is from Jacqui Newling, *Eat Your History: Stories and Recipes from Australian Kitchens*, Sydney Living Museums/ NewSouth Publishing, Sydney, 2015, pp. 56, 61.

6

GREEN SHOOTS

Syzygium luehmannii

Somewhere along the line, it seems, top chefs and
diners decided that native Australian ingredients
had become a déclassé remnant of the '80s and '90s,
something as shunned by three-star restaurants as
sun-dried tomatoes and sweet potato mash.

Australian Gourmet Traveller, 2010

In 2010, the Danish chef René Redzepi, the winner of
the San Pellegrino and *Restaurant* magazine's World's
Best Restaurant title for that year, arrived in Sydney.
He extolled the virtues of foraging. During a speech
at the Sydney Opera House to open the Sydney Food
Festival, he explained his cuisine: 'We are rediscovering

our region gastronomically ... We're very much with our wildlife, our wild plants, berries, mushrooms, wild animals.' He went on to suggest that this inclusion of foraged wild ingredients was essential to a cuisine: 'For me, I think this is the essence of a great cuisine ... It's a poor culture if it doesn't have a true, unique expression that can only be represented right there at the place.'

In off-the-cuff remarks, he admitted to being puzzled at the lack of native ingredients in the menus he had encountered here. The organisers of the festival did not need prompting. Accompanied by what the ABC television's 7.30 *Report* called 'a gaggle of food writers', Redzepi was taken to the Flinders Ranges in South Australia to forage for produce with an Indigenous family.

Reporting on this trip, one of that gaggle, writing in *Australian Gourmet Traveller*, assured its readers, 'Noma is the restaurant all young chefs are scrambling to work at' and predicted that there would be an outbreak of foraging for native ingredients. There was.

The imprimatur of Redzepi combines two assurances of success: the status of international celebrity chef, and the not-quite-dead Australian cultural cringe, a belief that nothing is worthwhile unless it comes from somewhere else (as seen with the macadamia). Redzepi's immediate influence was seen in such restaurants as Sydney's Stanley Street Merchants (since closed), whose menu boasted 'honey harvested in Neutral Bay to paperbark sourced on the streets of Marrickville ...

vegetables foraged or picked just hours before' and dishes like 'kangaroo, native fruits, herbs and spices; charcoal toasted meringue, ryeberries, ants'. Also at Charcoal Lane in Melbourne, in dishes like 'pepper-berry spiced cauliflower and quinoa cake', and at Orana in Adelaide, of whose food critic John Lethlean wrote, 'expat Scot Jock Zonfrillo is trying to fuse the spirit of Copenhagen's Noma with that of the Never-Never.' I doubt Indigenous Australian ingredients and modern, Scandinavian-inspired foraging and 'cooking' have been put together before as they are here.

It's easy to be cynical about the rash of restaurants serving native Australian food after Redzepi's visit, but I'm not. Only about the Australian food media's scramble to jump on board. Could this be just another 'food-ist' craze? (My definition of 'foodism' is an attitude to food and cooking dictated by fashion and the media.) It could well be the case. But for some time now there have been signs of change in the broader relationship between European and Aboriginal Australians.

Signs of the green shoots of grassroots reconciliation can be found everywhere. Green shoots only, but I note the changes in my own children's attitudes and understanding. They have Indigenous friends and colleagues – there were Aboriginal students at Sydney University with our younger daughter – and both have a far better understanding than I did.

I grew up in Kings Cross and Double Bay in 1960s Sydney. I didn't meet a lot of Indigenous Australians.

Not one, actually. If I tried to visualise them, I'd see warriors wearing very little but ochre and carrying spears. They lived in another world – way outback – in humpies. I would have agreed with Charles Darwin – who really should have known better – that they were 'a set of harmless savages wandering about without knowing where they shall sleep at night, and gaining their livelihood by hunting in the woods'.

The first Aboriginal Australian I met did a lot to dismiss my prejudices. Burnum Burnum was an actor, an author, a trickster and a philosopher who played first-grade Rugby Union for Parramatta. He would probably be best remembered for planting the Aboriginal flag on top of the white cliffs of Dover on 25 January 1988 and taking possession of England for the Aboriginal people. He was a friend of a friend, and the few times I met him he impressed me deeply with his humour and wisdom.

In an essay in the book *Race Matters*, Indigenous lawyer and activist Noel Pearson writes of growing up in a Lutheran mission in the shadow of the Bjelke-Petersen Administration, which was both ruthless and paternalistic: 'The increasing awareness that Queensland legislation and policies concerning Aboriginal people breached fundamental human rights, and that our mission friend [Bjelke-Petersen] was a leading and vehement opponent of Aboriginal rights, brought on a significant identity crisis for the community.'

Much later, and after ten years in court, what is

known as the Mabo decision on land rights was handed down. Pearson writes:

> for many Australians, both black and white, the
> Mabo decision represents an opportunity for
> the achievement of a greater national resolution
> of the question of Aboriginal land rights and an
> improvement in relations between the new and old of
> this land, a first step in a new direction which might
> yield the changes necessary for indigenous people to
> be genuinely repossessed of their inheritance.

But the challenge is still there, 'to negotiate the expansion of those rights without losing ground and without surrendering the chance of future progress in a struggle which has seen incremental advances but whose resolution is still long in arriving.'

As Gillian Cowlishaw writes in another essay in the same book: 'The struggles over racial inequality are no longer about segregation and exclusion, as they were in the past, but are fought out in a number of public arenas and institutions.'

That's not to say the old (or new) racism has gone, but now, from Mabo on, there exists the beginnings of a legal system which recognises that Aboriginal Australians were here first, and that they have prior ownership of the land. That is, at least, a legal and administrative victory. As Cowlishaw writes: 'Now that the non-Aboriginal legal system has offered something in the way of rights, however narrow, to refuse to engage in the game and to fail to appreciate the rules and its limitations – even if our purpose be to disrupt the game – no longer seems smart.'

How this filters down to the attitudes and behaviour of 'ordinary' non-Aboriginal Australians is yet to be seen. You can't legislate against racism, but you can marginalise it. And there are rumbles of goodwill.

In January 2015, there was a 50th anniversary of the Freedom Ride bus trip to some of the most racist centres in New South Wales, led by activist Charlie Perkins. This time, in Moree, instead of being met with violence and threats, they were feted by the mayor, other officials and residents. The local newspaper, the *Moree Champion*, reported the event on 29 January, citing elder Lyall Munro as saying, 'I'm afraid to say that although a lot has changed, a lot hasn't changed as well.'

One of the original 1965 Freedom Riders, Eddie Munro, was more optimistic. He recalled how he had been asked to give a speech in 2000 for the 35-year anniversary. 'I had been asked to give a speech and was up all night thinking about what I was going to say. Then, when I saw that welcoming crowd and compared it to the one 35 years ago, it came to me. I had to talk about how far we'd come.'

While writing this chapter, I came across this statistic: '20 per cent of respondents [non-Indigenous people aged 25 to 44] to a beyondblue survey still think it is OK to discriminate against Aboriginal and

Torres Strait Islanders.' That means that 80 per cent *don't* think it is. I read that as a large advance. The same survey found that 72 per cent believed that a reduction in discrimination was a priority.

This has to be balanced against a 2011 survey of academic staff in higher education reported in the *Koori Mail* that revealed that more than 70 per cent of Aboriginal academics and professional staff had experienced discrimination and racist attitudes in their workplaces. The academics especially described discrimination, tokenism and paternalism. So we're not there yet. But it's a lot better than it was a hundred years ago, when the views expressed in an editorial in the *Sydney Morning Herald* in 1838 (quoted in full in chapter 4) – that the Aboriginal people had no more right to the land than the emu or the kangaroo – would still have been the norm.

We can't ignore deaths in custody, the (as I write) attempted closure of up to 400 remote Indigenous communities, the appalling level of Indigenous incarceration (higher percentages than in South Africa in the last ten years of apartheid) – all this is shocking and I'm not, Pollyanna-like, saying there's nothing wrong; merely that it is slowly, very slowly, improving.

And then there's humour. Angelina Hurley, writing on *The Conversation* website in March 2015, asks 'What's so funny about Aboriginal and Torres Strait Islander humour?' And while the article offers examples from as far back as 1973, she notes – as I have – the huge success of the show *Black Comedy* on the ABC. Hurley asks: 'Are we giving permission for non-Indigenous viewers to laugh at us or with us? Having watched the show with great enjoyment and discussed it with friends, I would answer emphatically "with us".' She goes on to say: 'Comedy is an opportunity to bridge the gap. For it to be successful there has to be universality, something audiences can relate to. It should provide moments that continue to challenge ideas of privilege and identity in Australian society.'

Black humour is, and not in the expected ways, a funny thing. In discussing the show *Black Comedy* with a (white) friend of mine, he confessed it sometimes made him cringe. Me too. That's often the point.

Not just comedy, but also television drama like *Redfern Now* and films like *Charlie's Country* and the incredibly successful *The Sapphires* are bridging the gap between black and white Australia. And as the prejudice fades and the barriers come down, so too does our resistance to what, for many, was 'blackfella food'.

The *Australian Gourmet Traveller* article which suggested that 'native Australian ingredients had become a déclassé remnant of the '80s and '90s' also posited that 'there are notable exceptions – finger limes are a hot property, for instance, while the likes of marron, Murray cod and angasi oysters are in demand precisely, perhaps, because they're not marketed on the strength of being native.' Not to forget the macadamia. What if this is right?

This is a complex problem. These Australian native products sustained the Indigenous population for over 50 000 years. They were shunned by the colonists, and continued to be for over 200 years for a complex bundle of reasons, including what I've called food racism. But Australia is moving beyond the earlier racism and adherence to traditional European foods, and non-Aboriginal Australians are discovering not just tolerance, but the value of learning from and understanding the relationship Indigenous Australians have had with the land.

Interestingly, in my discussions with those chefs I describe as converts, as opposed to pioneers, I note their reluctance to make a 'big thing' out of using native produce. Rather, they treat it as just another ingredient in their dishes. They contrast this with the propensity of those I call the pioneer chefs to theme their restaurants around the produce. The converts are not hiding the ingredients, just not highlighting them. Is this occupation by stealth, or a more mature approach to Australian cuisine? Does it matter as long as we are at last using the ancient and fascinating foods that grow here?

Increasingly more is known about the First People of this land, often through European writers and historians like Bill Gammage, Eric Rolls and the rediscovered W. E. H. Stanner, but more and more through Indigenous writers, poets and artists. Writers like Bruce Pascoe, Alexis Wright, Kim Scott, Sally Morgan and Gary

Foley; poets like Ali Cobby Eckermann, Lionel Fogarty and Samuel Wagan Watson. And artists too numerous to list.

In an interesting postscript to the René Redzepi story, on 27 July 2015, *Travel + Leisure* magazine (and others) announced that:

> Chef Rene Redzepi, the founder of Copenhagen's famed Noma, will be relocating the restaurant's entire team to Sydney for a 10-week stint, set to begin in January. Noma Australia will be set on the edge of the water in the city's Barangaroo neighborhood, and will be open for lunch and dinner Tuesday to Saturday.

That will mean around a hundred people with their partners and children. It is something that Noma has done before, the last time relocating to Tokyo, where Redzepi added Japanese ingredients to his own Scandinavian cuisine. After the announcement, he arrived in Australia with two sous chefs, Thomas Frebel and an Australian, Beau Clugston. According to a report by Jill Dupleix in the *Sydney Morning Herald* Good Food section, they were here 'scouring desert, sea and sand for ingredients that might inspire the menu of Noma Australia'. Among other stops, they visited the Quarmbys (see the next chapter) and drove around the Adelaide Hills. It's to be hoped that this event will further influence the cause of non-Aboriginal

Australia fully adopting the native food – a process that's well underway with those farming and supplying the ingredients.

BEAU CLUGSTON
AND THE NOMA KITCHEN

....

SEA URCHIN WITH MACADAMIA NUTS
AND PANDANUS PALM

Serves 4

10 sea urchin (from Tasmania)
juice of freshly pounded rosella flowers
leaves of a young pandanus palm

Salt brine
20 g fine salt
1 litre filtered water

Macadamia nut milk
500 g green macadamia nuts
100 g seawater

Native pepper leaf oil
250 g native pepper leaf
750 ml grapeseed oil

1. To make the salt brine, heat the water and salt until the salt is completely dissolved and allow to cool. Divide the brine between two containers.

2. To make the macadamia nut milk, crack open the nuts with a nut cracker, remove the nuts and peel. Blend the nuts into a fine puree and pass the puree through cheesecloth. Thin out using the seawater until it has a milk-like consistency.

3. To make the native pepper leaf oil, blitz pepper leaf and grapeseed oil in a Thermomix for 7 minutes. Vacuum seal it in a bag and leave overnight to infuse the oil, then hang it through a cheesecloth for 8 hours or until just the pulp remains. Store the oil below 2°C.

4. Prepare the sea urchins. Cut open the sea urchins from the flat side with a pair of scissors and carefully remove the 'tongues', taking care to keep them intact.

5. Carefully dip the tongues into the first container of brine, and then again into the second, as the first container of brine will often become rather dirty. Reserve tongues separately in a container on ice.

6. Arrange the sea urchins neatly in a pile in the middle of a bowl, season them with salt and rosella juice. Slice the pandanus leaf stems (the white, juicy bottom 2 cm) into 1 mm thicknesses and place on top of sea urchins to completely cover them.

7. Finish the dish with a tablespoon of macadamia nut milk, placed around the sea urchins, and 7 drops of pepper leaf oil.

Beau Clugston is an Australian-born chef who has worked for six years with René Redzepi at Noma in Copenhagen as a sous chef. Beau was one of the team who worked at the Noma pop-up restaurant in Sydney in January 2016.

KYLIE KWONG

....

STIR-FRIED NATIVE GREENS

It was the René Redzepi talk at the Sydney Opera House in October 2010 which first made me, and many other chefs, sit up and take notice. Walking out of his talk, I thought to myself, what are we doing? Why aren't we using more of the produce naturally provided in our own backyard? The very next day I went about tracking down suppliers of native ingredients and working out how I could incorporate these ingredients into my menu at Billy Kwong.

Discovering native ingredients completely revolutionised the way I cooked at Billy Kwong, and after twelve years, such a discovery was extremely invigorating and exciting for me. Warrigal greens, saltbush, lemon aspen, samphire, sea blite, bower spinach, Davidson plum, quandongs and finger limes are just some of the native ingredients I use regularly, and their flavours are unique and incredibly interesting. At the point of discovering Australian natives, I began to completely reassess the whole notion of what Australian–Chinese food really was. I discovered that many of these ingredients worked in natural harmony with the Chinese flavour profile of salty, sweet and sour, and I am now very excited to be able to offer a truly authentic Australian–Chinese food experience.

3 tbsp peanut oil
½ tsp salt flakes
3 cloves garlic, crushed
200 g fresh saltbush leaves
2 tbsp organic tamari
3 tbsp chicken or vegetable stock
½ tsp sesame oil

1. Heat the peanut oil in a hot wok until the surface seems to shimmer slightly. Add the salt and garlic and stir-fry for 30 seconds.
2. Add the saltbush leaves and stir-fry for 3 minutes.
3. Add the tamari and stir-fry for 1 minute.
4. Add the stock and stir-fry a further 1 minute, then add the sesame oil. Serve immediately as part of a banquet.

Kylie Kwong is the chef and owner of Billy Kwong in Sydney. Her latest book is *Kylie Kwong's Simple Chinese Cooking Class*, published by Lantern (Penguin Australia) in 2012.

7

THE PRODUCERS

Solanum centrale

These indigenous plants promise a huge economic bounty for the country and our future prosperity demands they be given serious consideration.

Bruce Pascoe, Dark Emu

Marilyn Ryan is standing on a ladder beneath a lilly pilly tree, thrashing the branches with a long stick to send the riberry fruit onto the tarp on the ground surrounding the tree. The last time I saw this harvesting method was in Spain in the 1970s. That was how they picked olives back then, before mechanical harvesters.

But these trees and this fruit are in a very different landscape to those ancient olive trees I lived among in the mountainous north-west of Mallorca. As is the weather. It's January, the temperature is in the forties and Dennis hands out mosquito repellent. This is subtropical northern New South Wales, in the Nambucca Valley, 5 kilometres west of Macksville.

The lilly pillies are growing on Dennis and Marilyn's 43 hectare property, Valley of the Mists, which was, before they bought it, Dennis's father's cattle property. They've been growing and value-adding native produce here since 1989. 'We were classed as pioneers, as eccentrics,' he tells us. Because of the contexts and stories of this chapter – with both Indigenous and non-Indigenous participants – I have to point out that the Ryans are European Australians. 'When I started out, they said, what are you going to do? And I said, I'm going to grow native foods, and they said, you've got rocks in your head. You growing blackfella food, who's going to eat that? As a nation we're moving on and I'm so pleased.'

As well as lilly pilly, a variety whose riberries are seedless – and anyone who has cooked with them knows what a blessing it is not to have to deal with the tiny seeds – the Ryans grow a couple of varieties of finger limes, which are almost seedless and grow year round, four varieties of Davidson plum, lemon myrtle, and an aniseed myrtle that originated in this valley. 'It takes a while to grow, but what I like about this one is what happens when you put some leaves into a cocktail shaker with bit of ice and give it a working over and drop a bit of vodka over it.' Ancient fruit, modern use.

But there's a lot more to the Valley of the Mists than the produce. Their backyard is a 70-hectare wetland, officially known as the Hundred Mile Swamp, and home to around 117 species of birds, including egrets, jabirus and azure kingfishers. 'It's one of the largest breeding grounds in New South Wales for black swans,' Dennis tell us. And while it was once a freshwater swamp, Dennis says

it's coming salt now. Climate change, whether you believe it or not, is happening. These mangroves were never here, they've come in the last ten years. The salt is coming back up the aquifers rather than flowing out. The whole structure is changing – used to be paperbark and oaks, now it's going into mangroves and oak trees.

Everything changes. Probably 14 million baby sea mullet starting life in here, and prawns, they wouldn't have been here before – it's only accessible to the river in time of flood. We maintain it. No help from the government.

But the wetland does help the Ryans. Like many native produce farmers, they have more than one source of income. The wetland is one; they conduct tours on it. 'When things were going alright, Marilyn would bring a couple of buses in every week, from thirty to fifty on each bus. I'd do three canoe tours a week on the wetlands.' After the canoe tours, the visitors are taken to a shaded area to sit down for a taste of the Valley of the Mists products. Says Dennis:

> In the beginning, it was difficult because not a lot of people knew what to do with what we were growing. So what Marilyn did was to develop products using the produce we grow, over a quite a few years. We found the modern-day person likes to pour it out of a bottle, so that's what we did.

We also sat down in the open-sided shed that is the tasting room and sampled a few of Marilyn's creations. First, a Davidson plum wine vinegar. 'I make a wine out of it,' Marilyn says. 'It took me over twelve months to work out how to turn that wine into a vinegar. Beautiful with tomato.' And it is, with the Davidson plum's characteristic flavour, described in the *Journal of Sensory Studies* as 'earthy like fresh beetroot with slight pickled and chemical notes, with an intensely tart and astringent flavour.' Then a Davidson plum sauce, a finger lime marmalade and a macadamia nut chutney. And two dressings, a lemon myrtle and a lilly pilly.

Despite being hit rather badly by the GFC, Dennis tells us, 'with everything combined, we're doing OK.' And interest in native produce is picking up.

We're starting to sell more fruit. Still got a long
way to go. Clayton [Donovan, a local Indigenous
chef] seems to be very positive about it. [Other
restaurants] get stuff off us. They're more open and
they like to come and see how it's grown and what
we do with it. The younger people are stepping
outside the envelope. I think it comes from their
multicultural background – they're more open to
foods and doing different things.

I mentioned to Dennis the difficulty I've had finding
an Aboriginal name for the finger lime, a fruit which
originated in the rainforest in this region and which
is endemic from here to southern Queensland. 'What
we are forgetting,' Dennis offers as an explanation, 'is
that there were two generations [of local Aboriginal
people] that were basically zeroed, with alcohol and
whatever else. I've had the elders come out here and
I've taught them as much as they've taught me. It's been
a wonderful journey. They didn't know half the stuff
existed.'

In 2012, an Australian Native Food Industry Stocktake was undertaken by the Rural Industries Research
and Development Corporation (RIRDC) and Australian Native Food Industry Limited (ANFIL – the industry's peak body). It concluded that:

This Australian Native Food Industry is small, vibrant
and diverse. In 2010 farm gate production was valued

at between $15 million and $25 million and direct employment in regional Australia was between 500 and 1,000 individuals. Up to half of these individuals were Indigenous people living in remote communities.

It found that production takes place in all states and territories and that there is an equal number of tropical or semi-tropical species and arid or semi-arid species being gathered or cultivated. And although cultivated supply is now dominant for most species, mountain pepper, bush tomato and Kakadu plum are mainly harvested wild.

Producer and ANFIL director Rus Glover has divided 20th century involvement with Australian native foods into four phases.

We've had a sine wave of interest. It went through the bush tucker Les Hiddins syndrome, where basically everything he put in his mouth he screwed his face up [at]. Which wasn't good for the industry. Then we had the Vic Cherikoff era, where we started to develop an Australian native cuisine. Then, after a lot of national and international interest from chefs, we've further developed an Australian native cuisine. And now we're moving into a phase where some of our products are becoming mainstream – lemon myrtle is as mainstream as you're going to get.

Les Hiddins was a retired army officer whose show, *Bush Tucker Man*, ran on the ABC from 1988 to 1996. You can still see it online. Rus Glover is right. While he didn't do much to promote the cause of eating Australian native foods – it is reported, by Elspeth Probyn (in her book *Carnal Appetites*) and others, that off-camera he had been known to say 'he wouldn't eat that shit' – he did open his audience's eyes to the riches of the north. But overall, what we take away from these shows is that this is alien country; if you go there, you do so at your own peril. He offered a divisive 'them and us' view of outback Australia: there was no doubting his respect for the survival skills of the local people, but for Hiddins, they were from another country. Indeed, they were: their own. As Glover says, much has changed. And the change is fast.

The 2012 RIRDC Australian Native Food Industry Stocktake noted five producers along the north coast of New South Wales. At the time of writing, there are eighty-five. But rapid change and growth are not the only problems faced by this emerging Australian industry. Glover offers a conservative estimate of 5 to 10 per cent growth since 2012.

Amanda Garner, the ANFIL chair, was previously a chef and caterer and has worked with Neil Perry, Peter Rowland and George Biron, among others. Without putting a figure on it, she says, from her perspective, one product, lemon myrtle, may have single-handedly eclipsed the $15–25 million value put on the industry in the 2012 stocktake. 'There has also been enormous growth in wattleseed and the Kakadu plum,' she said. Coming up the outside is the finger lime, which is now being exported to Belgium, Germany, England and the United States. Garner recalls being in a meeting of the Pilbara Hinterland Agricultural Development Initiative (PHADI), who commented that the finger lime industry was the largest and most attractive they had looked at.

But with such a new, diverse and rapidly growing industry, there are problems, not the least being supply. Glover points to the issue of stockpiling. 'There are always people who want to take your product, but you might have to hang on to it for a while. Then there are the those who want it now and if they can't get it, they do something else. That's been the bane of the industry.' As it has been for the wheat, wool and beef industries. But Australian native foods face problems unlike any other.

Diversity, for example. There are now at least fifteen species of native Australian foods moving into commercial production that are being grown in every ecosystem in the country, by Indigenous communities, producers of other products – small producers with passion and little money. Glover points out that in New South Wales, there is now an officer in the NSW Department of Trade and Industry working three days a week on native foods.

Another contentious, even divisive, issue is the

various merits of the wild-harvested versus cultivated product. This is a complex topic. The issue is whether cultivation of a wild-harvest species can diminish the high levels of nutrients in many of them, including the Kakadu plum.

Research scientist Dr Izabela Konczak, who has spent some years studying the phenolic compounds and other nutritive components of native foods, especially the Kakadu plum, sees the benefits of cultivation. (Phenolic compounds are natural compounds that play an important role in cancer prevention and treatment.) She told me that the group she was working with for an RIRDC report was collecting fruit from different parts of the country and doing genetic analysis in order to match fruit quality with genetic background.

> The next logical step would be to select the best source – and why not try to make them better? This is where breeding can come in. For example, the Kakadu plum is a pretty small fruit and the stone takes about one third of the volume and some have very thin flesh, especially those from the Northern Territory. The stone could be up to 50 per cent in some fruits. We would like the fruit to be bigger, to have more flesh and maybe better organoleptic properties [the aspects of a food that are experienced via the senses, including sight, taste and smell].

But would this diminish the wild vigour? Dr Konczak agrees this is possible.

> Probably if we cultivate, the concentration of
> phytochemicals would be lost if we create very
> good conditions for the plant to grow. Why is the
> plant producing those natural compounds, those
> antioxidants? It produces them to protect [itself],
> so if we create very comfortable conditions for the
> plant, it won't produce them abundantly. I think
> the concentration might go down. But we might
> be benefitted, because the fruit would be easier to
> market and what would be left would be plenty
> because this fruit is so rich in phytochemicals.

Phytochemicals include over 10 000 compounds in
plants – apart from vitamins, minerals and macronutri-
ents – that have beneficial properties, such as immune
system boosting, cellular repair, and antioxidant,
anti-inflammatory, antiviral and antibacterial effects.

And perhaps in some cases there might be no
need to cultivate, but merely to look closer. Later in
this chapter, producer Pat Torres talks of a variety of
Kakadu plum in her part of the country that naturally
grows with abundant flesh.

Vic Cherikoff opposes cultivation, arguing that
intensive cultivation compromises the nutritional quality. 'As soon as you start hybridisation,' he said, 'you
minimise nutritional quality, unless the hybridisation is

aimed at maximising it.' He cites a Kakadu plantation in Humptydoo.

> They did all the right things, worked with an agronomist, selectively chose cuttings from fruits producing high vitamin C in the wild. They irrigated, put it in great soil, planted them out, and when the fruit ripened, the vitamin C went from over 3 per cent to 0.12 and 0.2. The trees produced beautifully, but the nutritional values were worthless.

Rus Glover has another view.

> There are other parameters that give you the difference between wild harvest and plantation produced. I do both. I harvest street trees when I've had a failure of my crop – lilly pillies are planted as street trees all over the north coast. I've harvested 2 tonnes from the street trees. It's a lot more work – can't do the nets and tractor in the street. The wild harvest is a cultural difference, but for nutrients availability – no difference.

But there is that cultural and perceived difference of the superiority of the wild-harvested fruit, even if there is no nutritional difference, and as yet we have no clear evidence on this. Garner believes that there is a difference, and that because of this

we need to formulate a system that certifies wild
harvest as being the premium product and make sure
that each individual fruit [from a farm] gets tested
and you have a sliding scale of nutrients. I think that
upsets your average horticulturalist involved in the
native foods industry, who says, do you mean to
tell me that my product is not a premium product?
The fact is that it's not going to be. There is no
way, at the moment, you can cultivate a product
commercially and have that same high level of
nutrients. That needs an enormous amount of
[expensive] research.'

But this does not mean a low-nutrient cultivated product is useless.

Extract from the Kakadu plum has been used to
extend the shelf life of prawns. University of Queensland researcher Dr Yasmina Sultanbawa has been
working on the natural antimicrobial properties of the
Kakadu plum, which can be used to replace some of
the chemical preservatives used by the seafood industry. Dr Sultanbawa told ABC Rural's Robin McConchie
that the seafood industry wants cooked prawns to have
a shelf-life in excess of fourteen days, and that Kakadu
plum tests have been extending prawn shelf-life up to
twenty-one days before spoilage.

This introduces another aspect of Australian native
foods. Says Glover:

The essence of understanding eating Australian is that for Aboriginal people a plant wasn't just a food plant. Take *Lomandra longifolia* (common name: mat rush). It's got an inch of edible starch in the bulb, you can soak the flowers and get the honeydew, it makes the best fish nets and dilly bags, and a leaf was used as a teething ring for Aboriginal children. It's not a dilly bag plant, not a fish net plant, it's a multipurpose plant. It's very difficult for other Australians to get some sort of understanding.

While it is outside the scope of this book, it should be remembered that as well as parts of a plant being eaten, the roots may be made into dye and the sap or bark used as medicine. As one of her Aboriginal colleagues, Banduk, told Jennifer Isaacs (author of *Bush Food: Aboriginal Food and Herbal Medicine*), 'All my foods have so many other uses.'

Medical researchers have more recently begun to examine Aboriginal herbal medicine. But when traditional medicine expert Dr Francesca Panzironi came to Australia several years ago to study how international legal standards related to Aboriginal traditional medicine, she was amazed at the lack of research or recognition of this 50 000-year-old body of knowledge. Panzironi said:

I had been aware that globally Australia is recognised as having advanced policy development and support

for traditional medicine, but it turned out this was
because of the official embrace of Chinese medicine.
I couldn't believe that there was a complete dismissal
at an official level of Indigenous health practice.

This is slowly changing.

Rus Glover has a breeding collection of 2000 lilly
pilly trees. He's selecting for certain traits and then
crossing those traits to get the qualities he is looking
for. Dennis Ryan has a red finger lime he's been prop-
agating to encourage the reduction of seeds. But to
return to the wild harvest/cultivated discussion, I'd like
to offer a short history of the tomato.

The tomato originated in Peru; the commonest
variety we eat, *Lycopersicon esculentum*, is one of nine
varieties of wild tomatoes still growing there. The
wild fruit is small (2.5 centimetres in diameter), red or
yellow, or occasionally white, with a sharp, acidic but
not unpleasant flavour. It was imported to Europe and
first appeared in Seville in the early 16th century. It
then travelled to Italy, where it was treated with sus-
picion. It was thought to be poisonous, an aphrodis-
iac and not terribly palatable. A contemporary Italian
herbal (a listing of plants) carried a drawing of the
plant with this legend: 'If I should eat this plant, cut in
slices in a pan with butter and oil, it would be injurious
and harmful to me.'

For many years, it was grown as an ornamental,
mostly in the gardens of the rich. The first recipe using

the tomato appeared in an Italian cookbook in 1692 in a recipe called 'Tomato sauce, Spanish style' – a very modern-sounding combination of tomato with garlic, onion, parsley oil and vinegar. From the 17th century on, it has been cultivated and improved. And behold the variety of tomatoes available in the 21st century.

That's 400 years of cultivation. We have been here on this continent for over 200 years, and have only been cultivating and attempting to develop Australia native foods – finger limes, for example – for twenty years. Other citrus around the world have been grown for 300 years, and every year thousands of new varieties come onto the market.

We have a long way to go. But with the number of farmers taking up the challenge of growing native foods, and the depth of research going into their uses and cultivation, the face of the industry is changing. Food and science journalist Julian Cribb believes there are over 6000 edible plants in Australia, most of which we have yet to discover. But we've left it so long, as the world wakes up to the quality of our native foods we may well lose them.

As they become mainstream, many believe (or fear) that Malaysia, Indonesia, Vietnam and China will begin growing them – it's already happening with lemon myrtle. The biggest supplier of rosella in the world is South Africa.

'I've just sent my lilly pillies to France,' Rus Glover said. 'They've made them into jam and brought it back

to Australia. And they've mixed it with French blueberries. I live in the middle of the largest blueberry
producing area in the southern hemisphere. And I'm
the biggest lilly pilly grower in the world. And I have
to send my fruit to France ...'

Since writing the above, the Bonne Maman Blueberry and Lilly Pilly Conserve has arrived, and both
Glover and I have tried it. When I asked him his opinion, he said, 'I tried it on toast and with ice-cream. It's
a really nice taste, a little bit sweeter than I'm used to.
I would have had more lilly pilly in it. I think they've
been very cautious. I could actually taste it, but I'm
used to the taste.' I agree. Not enough lilly pilly. The
unique flavour of the Australian fruit – spicy, with clove
and cinnamon notes – has been drowned in sugar and
blueberry.

As this book went to print, Glover had not been
contacted by Bonne Maman for more fruit. When I
contacted him, he said, 'We live in hope', and pointed
out that this is one of the trials of the fruit grower. He
also said if they did want more, he'd put in a plea for
more lilly pilly (riberry) and less sugar and blueberry.
In the meantime, all reports are that it is selling well.

Glover has tried for some years to find a major
manufacturer to process and market his fruit. The
approach from Bonne Maman came via one of his distributors. There is to be a major marketing push, with
lilly pilly saplings being sent to the food media. There
is a feeling in the industry that the Bonne Maman

jam may do for manufactured Australian native food products what Redzepi did for the restaurant business. There are a number of producers, and most, with one or two exceptions, are either farmers themselves, or have relationships with Indigenous groups.

One successful and long-established producer is Robins Foods, the marketers of the Outback Spirit range of products. Owners Juleigh and her partner (and ex-husband) Ian Robins began with a catering business and retail outlet in Toorak. One thing the Robinses always did was make their own jams and chutneys. And it was while doing this that Juleigh Robins began to question the ingredients she used.

> One night, stirring a pot of raspberry jam, my mind got to wander[ing] and I started to think about the food we were using and I asked Ian, do you know of any fruit we use that's Australian? And everything he mentioned, I'd say no, that's not Australian. And there was not one single Australian fruit or plant food that we could identify. That intrigued me.

> There isn't a culture of using these plants in our society. We haven't valued Indigenous knowledge and the foods haven't been part of our diet, so they haven't been valued either. For some reason if goji berries have a history in Chinese medicine, that's important. But Kakadu plums from up in the northern end of Australia [don't] count.

The Robinses have forged relationships with Indigenous communities through their Outback Spirit Foundation, which operates separately from the business and works with communities to establish agricultural programs and youth employment.

Another producer, Outback Pride, owned by Mike and Gayle Quarmby, is based at Reedy Creek in South Australia, 300 kilometres south of Adelaide. The genesis of their business was very different from that of the Robinses. As their website puts it, 'It was born from a need to take a positive journey following the tragic loss of a 20 year old son.'

Gayle Quarmby's involvement goes back some time. Her father was Rex Battarbee, a watercolour artist who met, befriended and mentored a young Aboriginal man called Albert Namatjira at Hermannsburg in 1932. Namatjira went on to become Australia's first famed Aboriginal artist. Gayle grew up with the Arrernte people and gathered bush foods with the locals as a child.

When they were deciding how best to move on after the death of their son, the idea of making a difference in the lives of young Indigenous people became their focus. Michael is a horticulturalist who specialised in the development of arid zone horticultural practices. And so they decided their combined knowledge could work for them in using the native foods industry to help provide jobs and training for Indigenous Australians in remote communities.

The Reedy Creek Nursery was the basis for this project. The core business of the nursery is native plant production for revegetation and forestry, which has resulted in a co-ordinated program in local communities which is the source of their raw materials. In his time at the Reedy Creek Nursery, Mike Quarmby has worked with around sixty-eight species of arid zone plants, testing them for commercial viability and ability to propagate. Of those, around thirty-five have been brought into production. He says:

> After we've propagated and trialled how long they'll take to come into production, [we look at] whether their herb, leaf or fruit value is of significance. A lot of plants that Aboriginal people used [happened to be in] season when they were passing through and [were] ripe at the time, but they're of questionable nutritional value. Or the actual volume of fruit or plant was so small, they were a top-up or a delicacy, but not commercially viable.

> In other words, there are an enormous number of Australian native food plants that were opportunist. They were just there, [but] of very limited value in relation to cuisine in the modern sense. I could name any number of species that are interesting and were used, but there are plenty of other things that are out there and are significantly better from [the perspective of] nutrition, appearance, production, etc.

For their purposes, the Quarmbys needed plants that could be grown by Aboriginal people for a profit and provide them with a wage. So they had to find the right plants.

> We travelled probably 250 000 kilometres the first
> couple of years with a GPS in the company of elders,
> mainly through the centre. We haven't really pursued
> the rainforest fruits and vegetables, because that's not
> … the primary purpose of the Outback Pride project …
> which was to help people in remote communities.
> I guess you could say we're experts in the arid zone
> area. It's an interesting thing that the arid zone, because
> it's been minimally disturbed in a lot of ways, has a
> lot more of the untouched native foods that happen
> to be there after it rains, or if it rains. That's been a
> sort of a preservation mechanism. Whereas around
> the coast, particularly if you're talking the south-east
> through the Vic–Queensland–New South Wales coast,
> huge numbers of Australian native foods have become
> virtually non-existent because of the settlement.

The other side of the Quarmbys' enterprise is the supply of fresh produce for the restaurant trade. But that, although an important way of spreading the use of native foods around the country in urban areas, is, as Michael Quarmby points out, 'a means to an end, to keep the project viable because we don't get any government assistance'.

The Quarmbys supply around 100 restaurants at time of writing, using nine distributors around the country – 'as many of those as possible are Aboriginal people, so we're employing them and their families and their extended families in the urban environment as well.'

> There's also a value-added arm to Outback Pride. We started the Outback Pride grocery business, which now supplies some 400 outlets across Australia. That meant a lot of these obscure things had to be put into conventional western-style sauces, jams, etc., in order to have a money return to the community. That was the biggest, hardest challenge I've faced.

The other challenge is working with people in the community who were not used to working. Years of welfare or 'sit-down money' has meant that for many, work is not something they're used to.

> The only other industry that is on these communities is the industry that Gayle's dad had started, the Aboriginal art industry. We went along and said maybe we could use his model and create another industry. Not everybody's an artist but [growing native plants] can get young people out of bed and get children, while they're going to school, to witness the role modelling effect of their brothers and sisters and parents getting up and going to a job, and that was the concept when we started.

The communities that the Quarmbys have had most success with have been those closer to main highways and facilities. And those with significant female administrative influence. 'Those with women who are chairpersons, those that are more led by the females, those are the most stable and the most progressive.' Michael Quarmby has a theory about why this is so.

It's to do with young men being influenced by pack culture. At the moment they get into lots of ice, sniffing petrol, dope and alcohol. Because the women often get pregnant very young, they get the levelling effect of having to look after children. They group together and that's what preserves their state of mind and makes them better leaders.

The Quarmbys have focused, in the communities they work with, on getting children to go to school.

A lot of the communities we've started, the bus drivers or the teachers go to the bush tucker plot to get the kids and what they're having is breakfast. And that's where they pick them up – they're having something to eat in the morning. It's very nutritional food and they're going to learn better, they're going to have [a better] attention span. The most important thing is that they can see the connection between building something to sustain them and the end result: that they get educated.

The Quarmbys are yet another example of people leading the way, using native foods in an attempt to revitalise Aboriginal communities and lives. Whether they succeed in the long term or not, Michael says:

> [It has been] very satisfying from a horticultural point of view. I get an enormous amount of joy from having planted 500 000 bush foods out on twenty-six remote communities, and in that process, because the plants in any particular community area were significant to those people, we had to work out how to grow those iconic plants for them in their gardens. The end result of that, we've discovered, is that some of [the plants] can really be quite special. That's broken new ground by force.

The Kakadu plums used by Outback Spirit are wild-harvested. Robins says, 'I work with a co-op of women, and each of those women [has] their own country and they harvest with their own family, and then they bring all the product together. We get quite lot of product from the Broome/Dampier Peninsula region.'

A leading member of that co-op of women is Pat Torres. Torres is one of the founders of Mayi Harvests, which describes itself as an 'ethical and sustainable Australian owned native produce business from Broome, WA'. Torres says they are 'mostly women. There are some men interested in the bush tucker area,

[but] because you've got a lot of native title issues, the men get pulled away a lot for the meetings connected to that. Political stuff. There are some significant men who are following the bush tucker line.'

Torres grew up in Broome, and started Mayi Harvest with a number of families.

It's a company, we have to buy shares – we're learning to do business in the western way. The bush tucker industry gives us a chance to utilise everything we know about the land. In the past it was difficult to know how to utilise Indigenous knowledge, because our knowledge wasn't valued. No longer are we 'the primitive people of the past'. Today, our knowledge is being valued.

Mayi Harvest cultivates using what is being developed as the savannah enrichment process, a way of farming which utilises the way the local people farmed for millennia. 'As our families walked and ate the fruit they'd bury the seed so it'd grow again.' This simple propagation method has been developed and transformed by local horticulturalists like Kim Courtenay from the Kimberley Training Institute (KTI) in Broome, working with the local people. In reporting on a trial of the technique in April 2013, the KTI reported that:

The aim [of savannah enrichment] is to transform a typical area of regularly burnt savannah dominated by fire tolerant species into a productive woodland/ forest with a higher density of long lived climax species – that is species that will eventually reach a state of equilibrium with their environment – that produce high value commercial crops and in the process to preserve and enhance local biodiversity.

It's a way of farming that not only avoids the pitfalls of monoculture, but improves country. Torres points to the examples of plantations in Kununurra,

... huge acreage of mangos and bananas that have serious monocultural problems. We think more in terms of enrichment planting, which maintains the natural bush and puts the fruit trees in between. Our people were very tuned in with healthy and sustainable living. Plantations tend to wipe the species out of the country. Each tree has insects, birds, animals that live on it and when we cut it down and replace it with a mango plantation that isn't even from here, it's from Asia, when you put that tree here, you don't have that ecosystem.

We're not thinking of plantations, but small family groups holding land, growing trees, creating more business all around with different bush food, and you put them all together. We're not interested in making a multimillion dollar business.

And as a valuable sidelight to the development of this technique, young Indigenous people are being trained in the technique and will be able to go back to their communities and start developing businesses.

The main tree being planted at the time of writing is the Kakadu plum, or, as it's known in the Jugan language (one of three languages in that country), gubinge (pronounced gub-inj). 'Gubinge is the product the world wants,' Torres says. There is interest in it from all over the world for a whole variety of uses. Not just as a food, but as a nutraceutical and in cosmetics.

[French cosmetics giant] Clarins came over to check us out. We haven't got a supply happening there, because we couldn't guarantee 50 tonnes of the stuff. They need significant supplies. At the moment our fields can only given us 10 to 20 tonnes, and a lot of that is being taken by people like Robins Foods.

Torres is interested in research into gubinge, but the right kind.

I'm interested in research to document the species. The DNA range is so vast, which it obviously developed for its own survival. You can pick up a good feed off this one tree and then it'll manifest itself in a different form totally. Along our coast you've got stunted trees – for example, a tree only 18 inches high gives 5 kilograms of fruit, and one

3 metres high, you're lucky to get twenty fruit off it. They call it the same species, *Terminalia ferdinandiana*.

Some fruits look yellow, some light white, some look green; some have got a little beak. There's so much diversity and what I'd like to know is, are they the same species or are they different varieties? Like grapes, you have different grapes – we'd like to be able to do that with gubinge. The pinks and the reds are the sweet-tasting ones; the green and the yellow are a lot tarter. You could develop a range for sauces and chutneys, and another range that go into plastic containers and go into supermarkets for eating. That's the research I'm interested in. Up in our region we have a big fat gubinge with a lot more flesh on it than the NT one. The seed is still large, but it's about a third of the size of the fruit. A good eating fruit that is already growing, with no need to develop cultivars.

But people keep going back to researching what can we make more money on. Let's make a cultivar, the cultivar can make us millionaires. I'm not interested in research that's going to take the taste and nutrients away. That's why we eat it – so we can remain healthy, not to have a nice-looking plant that can sell for a lot of money because it's reputed to have high vitamin C.

Listening to Pat Torres and Kim Courtenay talking about the savannah enrichment program, I'm reminded, again, that it does seem that some Australians at least are coming to terms with the country. At the end of *The Biggest Estate on Earth*, as I have quoted elsewhere in this book, Gammage writes, 'If we are to survive, let alone feel at home, we must begin to understand our country.'

Savannah enrichment and its merging of traditional knowledge and horticultural skills, with Indigenous and European Australians working together to create a low-impact industry of a remarkable Australian plant – gubinge – with a multiplicity of uses in the modern world, does seem to tick many of the boxes. When I discussed the program with Kim Courtenay, it becomes obvious that is exactly the way it developed.

Sydney-born Courtenay, an ex-journalist, now works as a horticulturalist at the KTI. The genesis of savannah enrichment lies in a program developed for Aboriginal communities in the Northern Territory to engage people using horticulture. 'In the metropolitan areas,' Courtenay says, 'colleges serve existing industries. Our clients don't have industries. Our training involves initiatives around developing industries that are going to suit the people we're working with.'

That idea itself had its roots in the mission vegetable gardens. 'From the very early days the missions grew fresh fruit and vegetables on remote communities as they did on the early cattle stations. This was rekindling the mission garden idea. The old people welcomed that.

They welcomed it because when, from the late 1970s, small Aboriginal groups began leaving the major settlements – often missions – to settle on homelands or outstations, this coincided with the beginning of the welfare era. Since then, there had been lots of people whose whole livelihood was based around 'sit-down money', and all the trappings that go with that. Courtenay says:

About 20 years ago we [KTI] visited some of the communities. They were saying, we need to do something to get out of the welfare mentality. And we began some wonderful relationships with the traditional owners, one man in particular, Merridoo Walbidi.

When I was in grade 3 at Waverley College in Sydney in the early 1960s, Merridoo, who's about my age, walked out of the Great Sandy Desert. His was one of the last family groups to come out. We've become great mates.

I began bringing Indigenous prisoners down from Broome to his Bidyadanga community. We started doing all sorts of things: planting trees, putting lawns in and then growing gubinge. I'd been interested in gubinge, Kakadu plum, for some time. When I said, 'Let's grow some bush tucker trees around here', Merridoo's eyes lit up. He said, 'I'll show you some of the ones from my country.' So we went down the track of incorporating the cultivation of traditional plants as part of our community gardens push.

So I'd drive down from Broome every week and Merridoo would be waiting with his crew, I'd have prisoners and we'd all get stuck in and do something. I nominated him for the Aboriginal student of the year in WA, which he won in 2004. When he was interviewed at the Parmelia Hilton, they asked him how he felt that modern culture and traditional culture could co-exist. And he said, 'We must walk together.' The two cultures walking together to create something that's going to find a positive way forward.

In the early 2000s, around the same time they'd put gubinge plantations in at Bidyadanga and several other communities, they made contact with a company called Coradji in Sydney, who had developed a business around gubinge. They were paying (at the time) $20 a kilogram for it, which was around seven times the price then paid for top-grade mangoes, a big plantation crop in the north. 'This reinforced our belief in it,' Courtenay says.

We formed a collaboration with other interested parties to maximise involvement with benefits for Indigenous communities. We had a meeting in Darwin and we were talking about cultivation.

And they said, 'We don't want to grow it using conventional monoculture because we're marketing it as a native fruit, which is a natural product. We don't want to use sprays and chemicals and fertilisers and all that sort of stuff.' So I said, 'At KTI we've got a block of land and we've developed a training and research facility. It's a site where we can do some cultivation trials.' We didn't want to see the land cleared, so we went about establishing the trees in the bush. And that was how it started.

In *The Biggest Estate on Earth*, Gammage showed what a profoundly different Australia it was when it was managed with what he called fire-stick farming. The roots of this go back to the time when megafauna roamed the landscape. And then, due to a variety of causes (still argued about by science), they became extinct, about 45 000 years ago. This event was followed by a huge increase in fire frequency on the continent. How were these two events linked? According to one theory advanced by Tim Flannery in *The Future Eaters*, it was 'the accumulation of vegetation which normally would have been recycled through the guts of large herbivores'. To counter the ravages of these frequent and cataclysmic fires, the Aboriginal people developed fire-stick farming, achieving a new balance which prevented the hot fires from stripping the soil of nutrients. As Courtenay explains it:

When you had people continually putting cool fires through from one end of the country to the other using fire-stick farming, you didn't have those holocausts nearly as frequently. And up in our area that practice maintained the parkland environment that Gammage wrote was created by fire-stick farming. Now we have less frequent but still very hot wildfires which have killed the long-lived canopy trees. Those fires have changed the landscape from woodland and forest to burnt savannah dominated by acacias, which tolerate fire, and quick-growing grasses. The fire-stick fires were probably more regular, but they were cooler, well-regulated and planned.

That was the eureka moment for Courtenay and his colleagues, when they realised that by putting cool fires through over a period of about four years, they had created the open parkland that Gammage talks about and eliminated these thickets of acacias.

Savannah enrichment, Courtenay explained, is a combination of reintroducing traditional burning to manipulate the country back into the open parkland landscape and taking it one step further by planting these high-value trees within that landscape to create productive woodlands. Drip irrigation is used to establish the trees.

In the savannah enrichment areas we establish our plants late in the year, we have the healthy young seedlings all ready to go, we have the irrigation in the ground and then we put the trees in to time with

the start of the wet season. We're on the fringe of
the tropics here and wet seasons can be hit and miss.
Irrigation gives us a guarantee.

As the process develops, there are plans to add
other high-value native fruit trees into the mix. Others
being considered are bush currant or black currant,
green plum or wild mango, and pindan walnut, the last
a relatively new discovery – by European Australians
anyway.

The savannah enrichment process is generating
support and interest at a time when people are looking to sustainable models for agriculture that preserves
biodiversity, unlike the colonial approach, which is
to clear the land, turn it into a blank canvas and start
again. By contrast, savannah enrichment regenerates
the land, provides employment and lays the foundation of business for communities.

'Merridoo and I share values,' says Courtenay. 'You
couldn't find a more traditional Aboriginal person,
and to have these shared values is encouraging and
empowering. It makes you feel you're on some sort of
right track. We're walking together. It's a tough time
for a whole generation of young people and we need
to provide some sort of hope and something that's
going to inspire people. It's a bloody interesting way
of managing this beautiful country of ours.'

Maybe we are, finally, beginning to understand our
country.

Pat Torres describes the future she would like to see, one in which 'all of Australia had proper partnerships with each other – horticulturalists have skills, permaculture people have skills, Aboriginal people have skills.' Torres believes there needs to be a joint system of management, where there's not excessive power control by one group over another.

> Just because an Aboriginal person doesn't have a
> Bachelor of Horticulture, it doesn't make them less
> of a person or less of a practitioner. There should be
> a recognition of the knowledge that our people do
> carry. Our knowledge is – what? – 65 000-plus years
> old? We know more about the land than any of the
> people who've come in the last 250 years.

If we're going to develop this kind of partnership between Aboriginal and non-Aboriginal Australians, then the question of ownership and meaning arises. As Torres reminds us.

> The plant is not just a plant. It has a huge role in
> the whole of our way of looking at the world. The
> plant is a totem, the plant is a relation, the plant has
> a skin group, it fits into a system of relationships
> with humans. It occurs in a particular season, it has
> a relationship with insects, birds and animals …
> including humans. It has a corroboree, a dance, a
> song and a paint. That's the sort of thing we're telling

the ANFIL mob. The wattle tree isn't just a tree where you gather the seeds, put them into a package after you've roasted and ground them. It's a lot more than that.

In addition to native flora, there are our unique fauna – animals and birds which are either ignored by most Australians or, in the case of the game birds, locked up behind incomprehensible conservation laws and, in at least one instance, regarded as a nuisance rather than cultivated for the magnificent table birds they could be. But just as this book was going to print, I received an email with some good news.

Richard Gunner is a South Australian farmer, butcher and provedore who deals in, among other things, game meats. He's always on the look out for new produce. In late 2014 he read a story about the impact magpie geese were having on the mango farms of the Northern Territory. These native Australian geese have fallen in love with the new crop and swoop on the farms when the fruit is ripening. Many farmers were shooting or poisoning them, and leaving them to rot.

Gunner sensed an opportunity. He knew how good magpie geese tasted and he knew he could find a market for them in the south. And he also had contacts with the Larrakia people on whose lands around Darwin were both geese and mango farms.

'We went and spoke to some of the people we know

who live in the area,' Gunner said, 'then went back to Northern Territory Parks and Wildlife and spoke to Keith Saalfeld, the person who handed out the permits to destroy the geese. In talking to this guy, it became obvious that he felt what we wanted to do was a good thing, but he hadn't found anyone who could do it properly.'

And here was Gunner with the expertise to take the processed birds to markets in the south, and with good relations with the Larrakia people – people like local AFL heroes Russell Jeffrey and Daniel Motlop. 'They were on-side,' said Gunner, 'and that helps as they've got the respect of the community.' Gunner was given a licence to take 4000 birds in the first year.

It was Saalfeld who came up with the idea of trapping the birds in 4 metre by 4 metre cages with one-way doors and food inside, rather than shooting them.

As Gunner points out, 'They'll be killed, plucked and processed by Larrakia people. This is a new enterprise for them. We're always looking for work that's not work, and for them this is not work. They love to hunt and pluck geese.'

In late October 2015, Gunner went to supervise the placing of the first traps. As with all new enterprises, there were teething problems in trap design and the bait used. The obvious bait would be mangoes, but according to Gunner the mango farmers don't want mangoes used. 'We're complying with their conditions,' he confirms.

As soon as the problems are ironed out, the first batch of processed birds will be flown south. Those first birds will be frozen, but as the business builds, Gunner will be able to deliver chilled birds.

It really is a triple win. The mango farmers are happy, the Larrakia people have a new income stream, and we'll be able to taste this magnificent animal, most of us for the first time. Let's hope this is only the first of a number of native Australian game birds to reach our tables.

CLAYTON DONOVAN

KANGAROO LOIN, PART-SMOKED IN LEMON MYRTLE

Serves 1 (for each additional serve,
add the same amount of ingredients)

This dish, with caramelised vegetables and a chocolate jus, is a favourite of mine. Those hesitant to try kangaroo have quickly changed their mind about it after tasting this.

200 g sugar
200 g rice
2 tbsp dried, ground lemon myrtle
1 kangaroo loin
500 ml reduced salt beef stock

1 cup red wine
bouquet garni (optional)
2 tbsp dark chocolate, grated
1 tbsp redcurrant jelly
olive oil and butter for frying
2 pre-cooked baby beetroots, halved
2 pre-cooked baby carrots, halved
1 pear, quartered
1 handful baby spinach
pinch of nutmeg
Murray River salt
dill and parsley, finely chopped

1. Mix the sugar, rice and lemon myrtle. Line a baking tray
   with foil and place the rice mixture in the bottom of
   the tray. Place a wire rack over the rice mixture, put the
   kangaroo loin on the rack and cover the roo and tray
   with a layer of foil.
2. Put the tray over a moderately high heat for
   5–8 minutes. Unwrap and turn the loin over, cover again
   and put it back on the heat for 2–5 minutes. Remove
   the kangaroo, place on another tray with a piece of foil
   tented over it, and keep in a warm place to rest.
3. To make the chocolate jus, first place the reduced salt
   beef stock and the cup of wine in a saucepan, with the
   bouquet garni, if using. Heat to boiling, then simmer
   until reduced to 2 tbsp. Add the dark chocolate and the
   redcurrant jelly and warm gently.
4. To make the caramelised vegetables, heat a pan and

add a little oil and butter. Add the beetroots and carrots and fry until lightly brown. Add the pear and cook until coloured. Add the baby spinach and cook until wilted. Stir in the pinch of nutmeg, and season to taste with the Murray River salt.

5. Slice the loin and pour some of the jus over it. Serve with the vegetables, with the dill and parsley sprinkled over the top.

Clayton Donovan is an Indigenous chef whose television program, *Wild Kitchen*, ran for eleven episodes in 2014 on ABC television.

RAYMOND KERSH

....

FINGER LIME, WILD LIME, LEMON AND QUANDONG TART

Serves 6–8

The first time I had quandongs was when I was staying at my sister-in-law's place at Yapunyah, close to Warren. We used to go to Mass every Sunday at Quombone and afterwards people would bring sandwiches and turn it into a social gathering: some people had driven from distant places to go to church. I remember someone offering me a tart that had quandong in it, and apologising about using this fruit. I remember thinking how strange it was to apologise for something that tasted so good.

Tart crust
150 g macadamia nuts
150 g pine nuts
150 g walnuts
50 g butter
50 g brown sugar
50 g dried breadcrumbs

Caramelised quandongs
½ cup sugar
3 cups quandongs, roughly chopped
½ cup red wine
1 lime, juiced
1 tbsp cassis or grenadine
1 vanilla bean
2 cinnamon sticks
3 star anise
1½ tbsp cornflour

Lime and lemon curd
½ cup wild limes
6 finger limes
150 ml lemon juice
zest of 2 lemons
50 ml orange juice
1 cup caster sugar
8 egg yolks
4 whole eggs
30 g butter, cut into small cubes

1. To make the tart crust, combine all of the ingredients in a blender or food processor and process until the mixture is thick and crumbly. Spread the mixture about ½ cm thick around the base and sides of a 25 cm flan dish, pressing the mixture firmly in place with your fingers. Put in the refrigerator to set.

2. To make the caramelised quandongs, combine all of the ingredients except the cornflour in a pan and bring to the boil. Simmer for 10 minutes, then remove from the heat.

3. Combine the cornflour with 3 tbsp of water to form a smooth, runny paste, and stir through the hot quandong mix. Return the saucepan to the heat and bring to the boil, stirring constantly, until all of the ingredients form a smooth syrup, with the quandongs still soft and whole in it. Remove from the heat, cool slightly, and pour into the prepared flan tin.

4. To make the lime and lemon curd, bring a saucepan of water to the boil, drop in the wild limes, remove immediately and plunge into a bowl of iced water. Repeat this blanching process, then set the limes aside.

5. Squeeze out the pearls from the finger limes and set aside.

6. In a small bowl combine the lemon juice, lemon zest, orange juice and one fifth of the sugar.

7. In a stainless steel bowl whisk the egg yolks, whole eggs and remaining sugar until fluffy. Place the bowl over a large saucepan of boiling water and continue to whisk vigorously until the mixture has a thick,

spreadable consistency. Whisk in the lemon juice, lemon zest and orange juice mixture and continue whisking until the thick consistency is regained.

8. Gradually whisk in the diced butter, finger lime pearls and whole wild limes.

9. When the mixture has a thick, smooth consistency, pour it into the flan dish over the quandongs. Leave the tart to set in the refrigerator for at least one hour before serving.

Raymond Kersh is the chef half of a pair of pioneer native Australian restaurateurs, his sister Jennice being the other half. This recipe is from *Edna's Table* by Jennice and Raymond Kersh, Hodder & Stoughton, 1998, pp. 141–42.

8

WILD ANIMALS AND GAME BIRDS

Backhousia citriodora

In the night they used to take dog, find possum, bandicoot or porcupine. That's the food we used to eat.

Bill Neidjie, from Old Man's Story, *as told to Mark Lang*

The little book *Aboriginal Bush Tucker of the Murray Basin* tells us that, pre-1788, 'Little wasn't eaten: galahs, pigeons, swans as well as ducks and other small birds.' Margaret-Mary Turner's *Arrernte Foods* offers those plus goannas, anteaters and ring-necked parrots. And not just pre-1788.

Barbara Santich wrote in her paper 'Nineteenth-

Century experimentation and the role of Indigenous foods in Australian food culture' that for many early settler cooks, 'Even the most unfamiliar and unlikely fauna became the subject of culinary experimentation.'

At least two of those cooks, Louisa Meredith and Mina Rawson, cooked and attempted to eat magpie, ibis, flying fox, bandicoot, echidna and wombat. Echidna, according to Rawson, was similar to suckling pig but 'too rich for most palates'; wombat was 'fatter and coarser with a strong rank flavour' but she appreciated bandicoot when it was 'soaked in vinegar then stuffed with sweet potatoes and onion and roasted or boiled'. Magpie was not a success. Louisa Meredith wrote, 'after exhausting all my culinary skill upon them in roasts, stews, curries and pies, I have finally given them up as not cookable, or rather as not relishable when cooked.'

There are, among those native birds listed, some we will come back to. But first, kangaroo – the most highly valued protein source for the Indigenous inhabitants, so much so that hunting techniques were developed just for this one animal. A hunter could and would track his prey for days, but was so often unsuccessful that a kill was highly prized, and the successful hunter gained great prestige. As with many food sources, the kangaroo offered more than meat. Flesh, bones and skin – all were utilised.

For the non-Aboriginal population, consumption of kangaroo has been contentious from the beginning.

The attitude of the first settlers ranged from grudging acceptance – at least until the next shipload of cattle and sheep arrived – to genuine enjoyment.

In her paper on the role of Indigenous foods in Australian food culture, Santich writes:

> It may have been partly out of desperation that colonists readily accepted and appreciated kangaroo – and its near relatives, such as wallaby – in the earliest years of settlement, but its resemblance in both appearance and flavour to other familiar red meats such as beef, venison and hare must have been reassuring.

She then quotes western Victorian settler Katherine Kirkland, writing in the 1840s: 'We often killed kangaroos, they are very palatable, particularly the tail, which makes excellent soup.' Others were not so entranced. Arthur Bowes Smyth, surgeon on the First Fleet ship *Lady Penrhyn* wrote, 'I have several times tasted the flesh of this animal ... but I cannot be so partial as to say it equals venison ... or that it is even as good as mutton.'

In the early 19th century, it was, in many parts of the country, a part of the diet of the colonists. As Australian environmental historian Nancy Cushing points out in her paper 'Meat for the pot', 'Kangaroo became a staple in Van Diemen's Land, issued in rations to convicts and free settlers alike for a decade from 1804 and ... the foundation for an entire way of life.'

Cushing cites the convict Michael Howe, self-proclaimed 'Lieutenant of the Woods', who 'dressed in kangaroo skin clothing, sewn with kangaroo sinew, carrying a kangaroo skin knapsack or Derwent drum, containing a notebook bound in kangaroo skin in which he wrote in ink made from kangaroo blood.'

But the reality was that for a variety of reasons, and for many years, it was shunned and has never been incorporated into the standard Australian diet. It was seen as only good for pet food, and, as mentioned previously, not made legal for human consumption in South Australia until 1980, and in all other states in 1993. It was considered dirty and diseased. Part of the problem was that the kangaroo was seen as competing with the imported stock: cattle and sheep.

Recently the kangaroo has been looked upon more favourably. Firstly, because of its light footprint it doesn't compact the soil like imported cattle and sheep. Secondly, because it is only 2 per cent fat. And thirdly, it has been revealed that its methane output is negligible compared to that of cattle. But still we resist eating kangaroo and wallaby. Not that there is a shortage of kangaroo meat.

As Cushing points out, 'kangaroos are killed in their millions each year under government supervised culling programs' – so many that it is 'the largest scale hunt of free living mammals in the world'. And then two thirds of the meat produced is exported. One producer, Paroo Premium Kangaroo, has decided to attack the problem head-on. Paroo is a subsidiary of another company, Macro Meats, who began marketing kangaroo meat twenty-five years ago. The reason for starting Paroo, according to sales executive Oren Hearnden, was 'to look at getting as many people as we could to try roo'. What had changed, according to Hearnden, was that 'we were living in a *Masterchef/ My Kitchen Rules* environment, where people liked the stories behind the food. And because roo had been portrayed as gamey – not very positive – it wasn't graded and it was [seen to be] all the same.'

So Paroo began exploring the idea of stipulating species for harvesting and discovering the best regions for harvesting kangaroo. As Hearnden told me:

> There are actually sixty-eight different species of kangaroo and we harvest four of those, and there are many regions. So we decided to focus on the best region in Australia. We went through and tried all the regions and species. We found the Paroo Darling region in New South Wales was the most consistent and the best.

The red kangaroo was chosen, as it had the most consistent flavour and texture. But then they came across the problem of consistency of supply.

> The one thing chefs and upmarket butcher shops hate is when they've found a good product and they

can't get it. What we realised was that the Paroo
Darling River is an unregulated river: four times a
year it floods. Which means the roos are scattered
and harder to get. So we looked for other regions
that had similar criteria to the Paroo Darling, so we
could ensure supply all year round.

They chose three regions to add to Paroo, the
choice being made on various grounds including feed,
resilience and pristine environment.

Paroo has gone to great lengths to tick all the environmental and animal welfare boxes, because some
environmental groups oppose the killing of kangaroos
for a variety of reasons which are outside the scope of
this book to examine. Their parent company adheres
to the National Code of Practice for the Humane
Shooting of Kangaroos and Wallabies for Commercial
Purposes. Their website claims they 'provide kangaroo
that has been sourced sustainably, responsibly and eth-
ically', and 'offer an excellent example of sustainability
through responsible use'. Paroo kill only male animals,
reducing the impact on the juvenile population.

One other area they are pursuing is an export licence
for the Chinese market, which is consistent with the
industry: 70 per cent of kangaroo meat is exported, to
Germany, France, the UK and, once again, Russia. Once
more, sadly, our native foods are more highly prized
elsewhere.

Another company using sophisticated marketing

methods to sell native fauna is the Tasmanian based Lenah Game Meats, who market wallaby to the professional and home cook.

There are other delicious and abundant fauna that, for various reasons, either bureaucratic or economic, are not on Australian tables. This may be the place to discuss just a few of them.

Australian chef and food entrepreneur Maggie Beer worked for some time to set up a market for the tiny (hare-sized) Tammar wallaby, which thrives on Kangaroo Island and which she describes as delicious. The reason these animals are not harvested, according to the Kangaroo Island Natural Resources Management Board, is that setting up an abattoir on the island to process the animals would be prohibitively costly in relation to the size of the market for them. There had been an abattoir, which closed in the early 2000s, and there has been talk of it reopening, but at time of writing it is still closed.

What is harder to understand is why we have largely ignored the unique table birds that could be farmed lucratively or culled sustainably (as with the kangaroo and wallaby) and added to the national table. Take the scrub (or bush or brush) turkey.

In her colonial cookbook, *Mrs Maclurcan's Cookery Book, A Collection of Practical Recipes, Specially Suitable for Australia*, Hannah Maclurcan gave a recipe for roast scrub turkey (*Alectura lathami*) which she described as 'a small bird, not much larger than a wild duck, with a breast like a pheasant and flesh as white. I have often served it as pheasant and people have not known the difference.' Clement Hodgkinson, author of the 1845 book *Australia, from Port Macquarie to Moreton Bay*, pronounced it 'one of the best birds for the table'.

But rather than being bred for the table they are seen as a pest. From 'Gold Coast Gardener' on an online gardening site: 'at present I am having a perpetual war with some brush turkeys.' 'Even more of a nuisance than its intelligence, though, is the brush-turkey's boldness,' writes the manager of BRAIN, the Brisbane Rainforest Action and Information Network.

Help is at hand. Pestecute, the Sunshine Coast Pest Control and Wildlife management company, will 'set up Brush turkey traps which are humane and allow us to relocate brush turkeys without harming them'. As mentioned in chapter 4, 'They brought their own', Jean-Paul Bruneteau told me, 'I just did what any Frenchman would do in a new place. I looked around for something to eat.' We looked around and found a bird and decided it was a nuisance.

The scrub or bush or brush turkey is found from Cape York Peninsula in far northern Queensland to Wollongong in New South Wales. This bird is listed as 'Least Concern in Queensland' (under the *Nature Conservation Act 1992*) and is ranked as a low priority for conservation action under the Department of Environment and Heritage Protection. Yet it is also listed as fully protected, as it is in New South Wales. Nowhere is it being cultivated or culled for the table, which – if, as is stated, its habitat is being threatened and as a ground-dweller it is threatened by feral predators – you would imagine would be a good conservation practice. But no. It continues to be seen as a pest. When we could be eating it with pleasure.

In a review in the *Weekend Australian* (26–27 September 2015) of a reprint of the Swedish biologist Eric Mjöberg's 1913 book *Amongst Stone Age People in the Queensland Wilderness*, Nicolas Rothwell quotes him as 'praising cassowary meat for its "very tender and delicious flavor".' Another untasted (by non-Indigenous Australians) culinary delight.

I've written about the wonderful flavour of the magpie goose. When I started this book, you could only eat it if you hunted it yourself. Attempts to supply this magnificent bird for the table had been unsuccessful. One of the most determined of those attempts was by Dr Graham Webb, the pioneer crocodile farmer. He wanted to set up a similar program to his crocodile farming (now a $30 million a year industry) for the magpie goose: 'The idea,' Webb explained, 'was to have a ranching program and raise them and pay the landowners for the eggs collected on their land, and then we'd raise them and sell them.' It ran into accreditation problems – for which read 'bureaucratic interference'. The cost of the research was prohibitive and no one, not even a government who one would have thought would be eager to set up such a potentially lucrative new primary industry, wanted to invest.

But now, as told in 'The producers' (chapter 7), someone has succeeded. South Australian provedore and supplier of game meats Richard Gunner has been successful in gaining official permission to take 4000 birds a year for the first year.

Yet another game bird worthy of cultivation and the table is the Australian bustard (*Ardeotis australis*), whose value as a table bird comes with the imprimatur of Captain James Cook, who recorded in his journal that 'it turned out an excellent bird, far the best ... that we have eat since we left England.' No surprise here, as it has been a valued food of Indigenous Australians for a very long time. They are listed as a threatened species in the Northern Territory, and endangered in New South Wales. As with the scrub turkey, perhaps the best way to save them is to farm and eat them.

The Cape Barren goose, another fine table bird, was cultivated for a short time, but failed, according to entrepreneur Chris Rhodes, 'because there were too many middle men. The cost of processing the birds made it unviable.'

Finally, the wonga (or wonga wonga) pigeon, again praised by Hodgkinson. He described its flesh as 'quite white and very rich', and goes on to comment that 'this bird has often furnished my bush table in the wilds of Australia with a "plat" not to be despised by the most fastidious gourmand.' Mrs Maclurcan included a recipe for this bird in her cookbook. A 'delicate wing of the wonga-wonga pigeon' was served to Godfrey Charles Mundy, the author of yet another book on Australia, *Our Antipodes; or, Residence and Rambles in the Australasian Colonies* (1855), when he dined with the acting governor of New South Wales in 1846. On sending this bird back to England, one member of the Acclimatisation Society praised it as the 'queen of the pigeon tribe … combining in the most delicate proportion the flavour of the pheasant and the grouse'.

I haven't even mentioned the twenty-one species of wild ducks which are only available to hunters and which could be professionally hunted and sold through game bird suppliers. Or the mutton bird. Or the crested pigeon described by Margaret-Mary Turner as 'very tasty'. I think of the mushrooms which grow in our forests and which we only began to eat in the 1990s – the saffron milkcaps, the slippery jacks – probably because migrants from Europe saw them and began gathering them. Now I can buy them in my local greengrocer. But these game birds are off limits either environmentally – when to eat them would probably save them – or because our bureaucrats just can't see the potential market for them. Australian chefs should be clamouring to have these birds on their tables. Without them, Australian native cuisine is incomplete. Now that the flora is beginning to be discovered, it's time for the fauna.

It is very hard to understand why these game birds, praised by the early settlers, have not become staples in the Australian diet. The usual objections discussed in this book just don't fit. Anglo-Celtic diet, food racism – nothing. It just seems like culinary laziness, a reluctance to move past chicken and imported duck breeds.

There is no doubt that there is much movement, much foment, much happening in the area of native Australian food production. But clearly there is more to be done. Whether we're on the cusp of an explosion of interest in, and consumption of, the food that grows where we live or it's just another sine wave, we won't know for a couple of years. But to this writer, who has been observing and commenting on the industry for twenty years, it feels like there is a change happening.

Making that change is not going to be easy. There are debates, discussions, agreements on rights and acknowledgement of, if not ownership, then knowledge, to be negotiated.

ANDREW FIELKE

....

BRAISED WALLABY SHANKS WITH OLIVES AND BUSH TOMATO

Serves 4

8 small wallaby shanks

½ cup flour for dusting

2 dessertspoons (dspn) extra virgin olive oil

1 dspn butter

1 large carrot, peeled

1 large celery stick

100 g kalamata olives, pitted

4 garlic cloves, peeled

1 large onion, peeled

1 cup (250 ml) red wine

1 litre beef stock

500 ml tomato passata or puree

1 tsp dried wild thyme (or a few sprigs of fresh)

1 tsp pepper leaf (or black pepper)

1 tsp sea salt

2 bay leaves

35 g bush tomatoes, chopped coarsely (3–5 mm pieces)

2 tbsp sea parsley, chopped

1. Dust the shanks with flour and brown all over in the oil/ butter in a braising pan.

2. Cut the carrot and celery into large (2 cm) pieces. Add to the pot, and brown for a few minutes, to caramelise them lightly.

3. Add the remaining ingredients to the pan. Cover and bring to the boil.

4. Simmer *very gently* for approximately 1½- 2 hours, until the shanks are quite tender, almost falling off the bone. The sauce may need a little reduction to thicken, if desired.

5. Serve with mashed potato, polenta or even risotto. Garnish with the sea parsley.

MARK OLIVE

....

MACADAMIA AND MUSTARD WALLABY STACK

Serves 4

500 g wallaby steaks, butterfly cut
1 zucchini, thinly sliced lengthways
1 sweet potato, thinly sliced lengthways
1 capsicum, cut into four equal pieces
olive oil
native mountain pepper
¼ cup crushed macadamia nuts
3 dessertspoons (dspn) seeded mustard
1 dspn honey

1. Pre-heat oven to 200°C. Coat the wallaby steaks with native mountain pepper.
2. Coat the zucchini, sweet potato, and capsicum with olive oil and cook on a hot griddle plate until tender. Sprinkle with native mountain pepper. Remove from griddle and set aside.
3. Sear both sides of the wallaby steak quickly on a very hot griddle until medium rare, then set aside.
4. On a baking tray, place a layer of the sweet potato, then zucchini, capsicum and wallaby, and repeat. Top with crushed macadamia nuts and place in the oven until the nuts are golden brown.

5. To make the sauce, mix the seeded mustard and honey in a small bowl. To serve, place the stack on a plate and drizzle with the honey mustard sauce. Sprinkle native mountain pepper around the plate and add some whole roasted macadamia nuts for presentation.

Mark Olive is a pioneer Indigenous chef, caterer, film writer and producer, educator and ambassador for Indigenous Australia. Mark can be found at www.blackolive.net.au.

9

CULTURAL CONUNDRUMS

Acacia victoriae

The wattle tree isn't just a tree where you
gather the seeds, put them into a package
after you've roasted and ground them. It's a
lot more than that.

Pat Torres

When discussing the question of plant ownership, one
of the producers I spoke to brought up the tomato. 'No
one asked the Peruvians if they could take the tomato
seed back to Europe. There was no question of ownership then.' The same went for the potato, chocolate
and all the other products of what is called the Columbian Exchange.

So who exactly owns a plant? Does anyone? There are differing viewpoints. After many years attempting to interest European Australians in the flavours of our native foods, chef Jean-Paul Bruneteau has come to a position at one end of the scale: that Australian native foods, as used in European kitchens, have nothing to do with the Aboriginal people, and should belong to the country rather than its original inhabitants. In my interview with him he said:

> I went on the SBS food show, we said this is about native plants and unique flavours: it's not Aboriginal. And they said we might need an Aboriginal person. I said no! This is not what it's about. Aboriginal people did not cook barramundi with lemon myrtle butter. They just did not do that. When you see [Indigenous chef] Mark Olive do all those lovely dishes with native plants it's automatically tagged as Aboriginal food. Take the tag away. Podocarpus plums. Riberries. Quandong. Wonderful stuff. Use it.

At the time, I found this a reasonable position. Now, I'm not so sure it's that simple. While Bruneteau is correct in that the ways European Australians use native foods often have little to do with the way Indigenous Australians used them, it does not mean non-Aboriginal people have no responsibility for their use. And there are many ways in which they can discharge that responsibility.

In chapter 4 of this book, I outlined the way in which, according to the book *White Flour, White Power*, 'rationing began to replace violence as a mode of government.' By deliberately interfering with the diet of the original inhabitants – as well as inadvertently doing so, through disturbing the land – European Australians destroyed Aboriginal people's health.

Having removed Aboriginal Australians from their food sources, they then ignored these foods for over 200 years. It seems to me reasonable that European Australians acknowledge Aboriginal ownership of these foods (as they do of the land) and work with them to ensure that at the very least, some of the proceeds of sales of the plants goes back to the communities. That's easy to say, difficult to enact. And ownership, as is always the case in dealing with Indigenous Australians (and other indigenes), is not the only question.

To take just one aspect of the relationship of Indigenous Australians with native food plants, let's look briefly at what, for want of a better word, we call totems.

As mentioned earlier, each individual in pre-1788 society had a totem which carried many responsibilities, the main one being to ensure the survival of that totem. A totem is a natural object, plant or animal that members of a clan or family inherit as their spiritual emblem. They define people's roles and responsibilities, and their relationships with each other and creation. On a higher spiritual plane, totems are believed to be the descendants of the Dreamtime heroes, or totemic beings. Even the humble maggot can be a totem – as Bill Gammage recounts, it is important to beliefs about creation.

The centrality of murnong to Indigenous culture is recounted in a paper by Fred Cahir, 'Murnong: much more than a food'. Among many other references, Cahir records a creation story of the Watjobuluk people of north-western Victoria: 'she [the sun] makes this journey; she is a woman who had a little son, and went with him to dig yams; somehow they became separated and she wandered around the edge of the earth up the other side.'

In his book *Dark Emu*, Bruce Pascoe writes that 'to deny Aboriginal agricultural and spiritual achievement is the single greatest impediment to inter-cultural understanding and, perhaps, Australian moral and economic prosperity.' While I don't believe that any of the protagonists in the field would argue that we should or even could return to pre-1788 culture, what is being worked towards are systems whereby Indigenous participation in harvesting and growing is recognised and rewarded, and both parties in the industry – Aboriginal and European – work together, or, in the memorable phrase of Merridoo Walbidi, walk together.

On a more practical level, in her 2010 Barrgana lecture, Pat Torres said, 'We don't exclude people. We look for partnerships. Hopefully by sharing the food and sharing the stories we'll create an understanding, they'll want to invest in us.' But in this complex and litigious 21st century, there needs to be a binding legal framework around the relationship, and the moral rights to the plants.

The Indigenous business community itself is aware of this. Aboriginal Bush Traders – a not-for-profit Indigenous community organisation which operates in many arenas, including bush-harvest products gathered by local communities – publishes on its website a comprehensive 'guide for Aboriginal knowledge holders on recording and commercializing Aboriginal plant knowledge'. It gives advice on legal issues such as:

> If you think you might have knowledge that only
> you and your community know about, it is important
> to keep it secret. If you can't help telling somebody
> about a particular plant and how it can be used
> therapeutically or medicinally, let them know that
> what you are telling them is 'confidential', and if
> possible have them sign a confidentiality agreement.

There is advice on employing field researchers, once again ensuring that all discussions are treated as 'commercial in confidence'; confirming that plants taken back to a laboratory for research comply with the Convention on Biological Diversity; ensuring that any plant resources from the wild in the Northern Territory comply with the benefit-sharing agreements of the *Biological Resources Act* of the Northern Territory; and other ethical and moral issues, including the possibility of the use of genetic material leading to a patent.

Just this one document on the website is twenty-two pages of small print plus a two page bibliography. Anyone thinking they can march into the bush in the Territory and walk out with a bunch of plants will do well to think again. But that is what has happened in the past.

In January of 2011, RIRDC published 'Indigenous fair trade in Australia: scoping study', which was an attempt to outline ways in which products and services from Aboriginal communities can be recognised and identified, and traditional knowledge protected. It was aimed at everybody working in the native produce industry, and 'people in the supply chain for products and services from communities, people working in fair trade, certification bodies or government policy'.

The study is remarkably thorough, outlining the procedure for following the Fairtrade path, or for creating an Authenticity Mark, a less formal process than Fairtrade. The pitfalls are outlined and case studies cited.

One of those case studies was the attempt (ultimately successful, as it has turned out) of the American Mary Kay cosmetic company to hijack ownership and disregard Indigenous knowledge to patent the use of kakadu plum extract in one of its cosmetics, a legal battle that was going through the courts at the time of publication of the report. In searching for information on this case, I came across an advertisement for a Mary Kay product called 'TimeWise Replenishing Serum+C', whose ingredients include Kakadu plum extract.

The story of this patent application shows the difficulty faced by traditional owners. Mary Kay failed to win patent rights in Australia in 2010. When they applied for that patent, according to a release from the Gundjeihmi Aboriginal Corporation (GAC), 'The company has never consulted Aboriginal people to discuss a benefit-sharing arrangement despite developing and retailing products that utilise their intellectual property.' Having failed in their bid for an Australian patent, they went back to America, and won a patent for one of the chemical constituents in the Kakadu plum. The release went on to say, 'This cavalier pursuit of profit over principle undermines Mary Kay Inc's claims to corporate social responsibility.' Sadly, that sounds like business as usual.

The GAC is not giving up without a fight. They've retained Sydney Indigenous intellectual property lawyer Terri Janke to advise and are working with others to see what can be done. Ms Janke has fired a shot across the bows of Mary Kay by reminding them of 'boasts [about their] work promoting women's rights' and that this action has 'potentially disrupted positive Indigenous socioeconomic opportunities in north Australia, including at the Wadeye women's centre, which operates a Kakadu Plum wild harvest industry'.

As the scoping report stated, 'the awareness of the

patents [which had been applied for] reinforced the determination ... that caution should be exercised in the disclosure of special knowledge of bush foods.'

Another cautionary tale in the report tells of a 'Northern Territory participant with expertise [in growing Kakadu plum]' who had worked with an American company on the development of commercial plantations which would be more sustainable and efficient than wild harvest. The local went ahead with this believing he was helping to develop Indigenous enterprises that would have benefitted the traditional owners – only to be told by his 'partner' that the parent company had decided it made more economic sense to grow in Brazil.

Of course, Mary Kay and the businessman from Brazil were not the first to rip off Australian native produce. The well known case of the macadamia nut taking American nationality in Hawaii was perhaps the first such case. As lilly pilly grower Rus Glover reminded us, when a food plant becomes mainstream, it will be grown in Asian countries like Malaysia, Indonesia, Vietnam and China. We need to safeguard our natural resources.

Another contentious cultural issue is, curiously enough, what we call these foods. When I talk about them with Aboriginal people, they use the term 'bush foods' or 'bush tucker'. But the report tells us that 'industry strategy today is to be identified by the term "native" as opposed to "bush" foods in an attempt to rid itself of identification with survivalist conceptualization of bush tucker, as well as the less appetizing food items to many Australian palates such as the witchetty grub.'

Pioneer native produce chef Jean-Paul Bruneteau has a similar view to the industry, with one difference. When he opened his first restaurant, Rowntrees, in 1984 with business partner Jennifer Dowling, he wanted to call it an Australian restaurant. In the telephone book, it was billed as 'International Cuisine', and the Yellow Pages told him it couldn't be called Australian because there was no such thing. 'And we said, well there is, so get with it.' They won. Rowntrees was the first restaurant to be listed as Australian. Bruneteau believed if he could be listed as an Australian restaurant, 'we'd get Australian cuisine too.' But that proved more difficult:

> I couldn't get the Australian cuisine thing across. It
> was always 'bush tucker'. I let it go a few times then
> eventually I would stipulate to the journalist, please,
> whatever you do, this is an Australian cuisine, not
> bush tucker. And it always came out as bush tucker.
> Bush tucker is about collecting food in the bush and
> eating it in the bush. I was using Australian native
> foods, plants that grew in Australia that had different
> flavours. These were new ingredients, the newest
> oldest ingredients on earth.

This will change. Indeed, is changing. Radio National's PM news digest on 18 May 2015 carried an item covering many of the issues I've written about here, issues I have never seen in the mainstream media before. Both Pat Torres and Kim Courtenay were interviewed on the surge of interest in gubinge, and what that means economically and for the Indigenous people of the north. 'There's no doubt it is going to be an industry,' Courtenay was quoted as saying, 'and I guess our priority is making sure it's an industry that does give local people the most benefits.' A refrain taken up by Pat Torres: 'So much has been taken from Indigenous people, and this is one of the few things left where we can do business with it because we understand the tree, we understand the seasons, we know how to protect it, we know how to collect the fruit.'

The most important change in the native food industry, one that has been talked about for a very long time, is the attention being given to the needs and the rights of the custodians of the land on which the foods are grown. This needn't be a restriction. It should be a spur. Because working – and walking – together, European and Indigenous Australians can pool their knowledge to harvest better, market better – and cook better.

TONY BILSON

....

JELLY OF BOTANY GREENS WITH SEA URCHIN ROE AND NATIVE LIMES

Serves 4

We use native foods all the time, seafood being the greatest example. What we've done is adapted things that were more familiar to the European settlers. While a lot of the fish were unfamiliar to the English, we have a lot of the fish they use in Marseilles, so when the French were out here they thought they were in heaven. Red rock cod, daurade, john dory – we're one of the few places in the world to have all those fish.

I went to Arnhem Land in 2011 for the One Laptop Per Child group. They asked me to do a dinner inspired by the food I saw there, which we did. Djawa Burarrwanga, a member of the Gamatj clan and chairman of the Yirrkala Dhanbul Aboriginal Corporation, adopted me as his father. I said, 'Why not your brother?' and he said, 'You're too old!'

Laklak, Djawa's mother, took me out and showed me a lot of the plants. We did a cooking session where I made bread and various things. We went out fishing together. Out of that came the dishes we did for that dinner.

Up there, they use things like, for example, the liver of the stingray, which is very like foie gras. They take the gut of the kingfish and pound up the flesh with one third of the liver and make a sausage out of that, which they then cook at the bottom of the fire, 65–75° Celsius for about 6 hours. Like sous vide. And then they roll it in the ashes and cool it. They use that for food when they're out hunting. It was fantastic. I've used stingray liver, and the French use it. The Yolnu only use it at a particular time of the year when it's very fat. They also tend to eat their game very rare – another similarity with the French. When they cook magpie geese, they have them rare.

500 g snapper heads, sawn in quarters
15 g chopped shallot
¼ chopped onion
½ chopped carrot
1 stick celery, chopped
1 sprig thyme
5 parsley stalks
zest of ½ lemon
zest of 1 lime
5 peppercorns
500 ml white wine
1 litre water
8 g salt
2 leaves of gelatine, soaked
1 bunch spinach
1 bunch French tarragon
½ bunch flat parsley
½ bunch basil
sea urchin roe
salt crystals
6 finger limes

1. Soak the snapper in salted ice water overnight, then wash in running water until all traces of blood have been washed away.

2. Soften the mirepoix (the mixed chopped shallot, onion, carrot and celery) in a little olive oil over a low flame without colouring them.

3. Add the washed snapper heads, thyme, parsley stalks, lemon and lime zests, peppercorns, white wine, water and salt. Bring to 80°C and keep at that temperature for two hours. *Note: do not boil.*

4. Strain through muslin. Stir in the gelatine. Refrigerate, skimming the fat off the top when it has cooled.

5. Wash and pick the spinach, French tarragon, parsley and basil. Blanch and refresh them. Press all water from the greens, puree them, then pass them through a fine sieve.

6. Mix the puree of greens into the snapper jelly.

7. To serve, allow 30 ml of the jellied greens per portion. Place two tongues of urchin roe on top of each portion. Garnish with salt crystals and finger lime pearls.

10

THE CHEFS:
PIONEERS AND CONVERTS

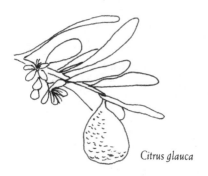

Citrus glauca

I'm not going to fill my menu with native ingredients.
I want to incorporate them with all the other
ingredients we have and be proud of all that produce
as much as the native ingredients.

Peter Gilmore, convert

The first Aboriginal chef I met was Tasmanian Chris
Jackman. It was 1998, and I asked him for some recipes for a project I was working on. I had heard about
him before I met him, from George Haddad. Jackman
was cooking for Haddad in his then highly regarded
Hobart Lebanese–Australian restaurant, Ali Akbar. Of

Jackman, George said, 'I don't think you meet two like Chris in a lifetime – if you do, you're bloody lucky.' When I spoke to him, he had his own highly regarded restaurant in Hobart, Mit Zitrone.

The recipes arrived with a carefully handwritten document which is so evocative and telling that I am going to reproduce it here, almost in its entirety, for the first time. And I will also reproduce one of his recipes – the only one that contained an item of native Australian produce:

I was born in Hobart in 1969 and grew up on the family farm in Collinsvale, 30 minutes from Hobart following the Mount Wellington Range.

As children, we were expected to maintain the land. The whole family worked together. We did most things by hand such as making our own fence posts and building the sheds for the animals.

We kept many animals. Geese, ducks, turkeys, chickens etc. These we killed to eat and sell. My mother made cakes from the eggs, even from the very large and rich goose eggs. My mother milked the cows and made cream and butter both for us and to sell. She also made the bread. We helped. My father bought the local bus and would, in the mornings and the afternoons, pick up and deliver the children. This worked really well as the poultry, eggs, cream and butter would be packed ready in the bus to sell to awaiting parents.

We slaughtered our own sheep and other life stock. The sheep would hang in the shed wrapped in old bed sheets. Once hard we would help process them. My father used an old wood saw to saw them in half on the verandah.

My mother always had projects. We fattened pigs with the neighbours and made from them hams, bacon and sausages. The sausages were made by mincing the belly through a hand mincer. The mince, piled into the centre of an old kitchen table, was seasoned and flavoured with herbs, taste tested, then once again minced into washed intestines.

My parents loved to do everything by hand. For a while we grew and crushed our own grain. The 1930s Morris truck was backed up to the shed and a belt ran from the tyre to the grain crusher. The truck locked in gear and a brick on the accelerator we had one fast grain crusher. It was great to have bread made from that grain and to also know that mixed with water the chickens ate it too.

Food at home was usually simple but home grown and processed by hand. I suppose that the food I like to create has been forged by the childhood I had. I love to make everything by hand and after working at such great restaurants as Stephanie's, Paul Bocuse, Capers, The Battery Point Brasserie, I have learnt the skills to produce fine food.

Stephanie Alexander would have to be my most favourite chef of them all. Her love for fine food, her knowledge of flavour – flavour always comes first with Stephanie – and such a natural touch with everything she creates. I found it difficult to work with Stephanie, I think because I admired her so much and I always became nervous when she was around. In turn this made her nervous as well. I never wanted to do anything wrong in her presence.

Mit Zitrone to me is a very simple and natural restaurant. Everything has been made by hand by myself my friends and my family. We made the tables and the lamps, we painted and even built the bar and the kitchen benches – a lot of thought and planning. The food is the same – very simple but made by hand with thought and care.

Chris Jackman died in 2012 at the age of forty-three. The powerful story he tells above adds to the long list of those which redefine European Australian preconceptions of Aboriginal people. It's futile to speculate on the direction his food might have taken him had he lived longer. But knowing his pride in his origins and his restless creativity, I'd like to think he would have embraced the food of his land in the new wave of interest created around the time of his death.

But to return to that first burst of enthusiasm for native produce from the chefs of the time, let's be thankful that a young Frenchman arrived here with a curious palate.

Jean-Paul Bruneteau arrived in Australia at the

age of twelve in 1967. He was born at Les Sables-d'Olonne on the French west coast, south of Brittany. He grew up eating the fish caught by the local fish-ermen, and mushrooms, chestnuts and snails foraged from the surrounding countryside. His grandmother Aimée, mother Denise and aunt Paulette were all fine cooks, preservers and bottlers. There was a family vineyard. Among the many vegetables grown by his uncle Pierre was what was called in France tetragon – the warrigal greens Jean-Paul discovered in his uncle's garden in 1989, when he and his business partner Jen-nifer Dowling went to France and visited his family.

I love that story of Bruneteau discovering that a food that he had eaten as a child in France was actually Australian. It speaks to our culinary cringe and to our ignoring what literally grows beneath our feet.

The future chef's first cooking job was flipping burgers at a milk bar. He did a chef apprenticeship, joined the navy as a cook, and at twenty-three became the youngest chief cook in the merchant navy. But it was on shore leave in New Zealand that the seeds of his cuisine were sown.

> I remember these women who stayed with us said,
> 'We're going to go and pick some wild foods', so I went
> out with them and they were picking this and that and
> I thought – the Aborigines – what did they eat? I did
> the research and found all the descriptions are there
> and the flavours – and that's what sparked me.

Bruneteau and Dowling opened their first Australian cuisine restaurant in 1984. And that coincided with the activities of another migrant son, Vic Cherikoff.

Cherikoff's mother was from Harbin, near Moscow, and his father's grandparents 'walked across Russia into China. I ate Chinese food from an early age. I grew up eating duck's feet, and gizzards, and my Russian heritage fed me sour cream and beef stroganoff.' At high school he went bushwalking, nibbling as he went. 'I was eating stuff and not knowing what I was eating: just tasting and spitting.'

The experimental nibbling was given authority via several degrees: science, oceanography, environmental biology and biochemistry. And then, in 1983, the grant for a job he had working in clinical pharmacology, which involved collecting marine bivalves, ran out. His wife showed him an ad for a job analysing wild foods. He got it after including in his application a list of all the wild foods he had identified while bushwalking.

This position was with the University of Sydney's Human Nutrition Unit under Dr (now Professor) Jennie Brand-Miller. He was to go into the field, harvest wild foods, analyse them for their components and communicate the information to various organisations, including the Northern Territory Department of Health and the Central Australia Dental Service.

It was during this period of harvesting and analysis that Cherikoff and his team learnt of the massive amounts of vitamin C in the Kakadu plum/gubinge. At the time, Cherikoff recalls, 'academia slammed us, Les Hiddins and Keith James [another native foods researcher] said it was total bullshit.' Today we know, through extensive research by RIRDC and CSIRO (cited in chapter 2, 'Home-grown marvels'), that the 'Kakadu plum contains the highest recorded levels of vitamin C of any plant in the world.'

In 2000, Cherikoff took me for a foraging trip into a nondescript patch of sclerophyll forest alongside a busy section of Pittwater Road. Two hundred metres in from the road and we're surrounded by edible plants, ready to eat or waiting for their season. There's a lily called dianella, with sweet, blue berries. From the sarsaparilla plant, you eat the sweet young red leaves, which taste like liquorice, cola, aniseed – a sensational flavour. It also has, Cherikoff says, a mild stimulant effect. It would make a wonderful salad leaf or a tea. In a patch of plain old Sydney sclerophyll scrub, Cherikoff found at least fifteen edible plants, berries or tubers.

Vic Cherikoff maintains his belief in Australian native foods, most especially those harvested from the wild, and his reasons for doing so have more to do with nutrition than taste. He offers a radical view of the future:

Years ago I was camped out at place called Wutan, up near Aurukun, where the Archer and the Watson rivers join together. An Aboriginal man I met there told me that many elders believed the time of the Aborigine will be back again and the whites will become extinct – they're waiting for us to die out. Now, as long as wild foods survive and Aboriginal people forage and go back to a traditional lifestyle – there may be something in it. We're getting nutritional diseases, 70 per cent of the reason we go to the doctor these days has a nutritional basis – we're only supported by good medicine and that's becoming more and more expensive. We're probably going to have to produce 70 per cent or more food and the only way to do that is through manipulation and the rubbish food we're growing now. We can't survive on that – it'll fill your belly for a while and it'll cause more nutritional problems and more people will die earlier. Wild foods are the key to reversing a lot of the damage done by our modern diet.

And how did Cherikoff get together with Bruneteau?' 'One of my diving mates told me there was an Australian restaurant in Hornsby [Rowntrees]. And I had a freezer full of wild foods that had been stabilised – brilliant flavours. Fruit, tubers, a whole bunch of things.'
And Bruneteau was ready:

The first thing I wanted to do in the restaurant was to serve the ultimate native food: a witchetty grub.

I'm a snail-eating Frenchman – there was a similarity.
I put a note in *The Land* (a rural newspaper) looking
for tenders and got quite a few calls. A bloke called
Bruce Henley became our source, and I got some
local press very quickly. A local journalist came and
she got us a story in the *New York Times*. Then it made
the BBC, the *Los Angeles Times*, we had NBC's Bryant
Gumbel – and that was when Vic came along. He
said 'I've just read about you. I've got all these foods
and would you like to try them?' We paid Vic a
retainer to supply us with ingredients.

Thus began a period of intense experimentation,
success and failure. Here was a young chef taking these
often alien ingredients into his kitchen and working
out how to incorporate them into his French-based
cuisine. There was little or no precedent, no road map,
no one to ask for advice. He was on his own.

The first ingredient to be put under the kitchen
microscope, Bruneteau remembers, was the wattleseed.

I stored it on the shelf for a year and kept smelling
it. I thought, this smells like coffee. You can't put it
with fish, or meat – I couldn't get my head around it
until one day we roasted it and ground it and put it
through Vic's Atomic coffee maker – and I thought,
oh my God, this is magic. We went out and bought
three tons of the stuff.

You'll find Bruneteau's recipe for rolled wattleseed pavlova in this book (see page 96).

From the beginning, he knew it was working. 'I was sure we were on the right track to develop this cuisine. I thought these flavours are unique, this is just Australian.'

But it wasn't all as easy as wattleseed. There were some – like the Illawarra plums – that weren't that straightforward. 'You have to heat them and cool them down to get the flavour. I tasted them and thought, this isn't going to work, and then I put them in the fridge and tasted them again and, thought this is amazing.'

Riberries, he discovered, need treatment with sugar and are resilient. Once, he left the entire seasonal batch cooking for 'the best part of 45 minutes' while he was on the phone. The liquor had almost evaporated, but 'after cooling overnight, the fruit regained its vigour and retained its full flavour.' 'The riberry is an exceptionally flavoursome fruit and epitomises the versatility of Australian wild foods,' he wrote in *Tukka*, a book worth looking for. It details Bruneteau's experiments, offers knowledge, history and Aboriginal food lore, and contains many of his ground-breaking recipes.

In 1991, he opened Riberries in Surry Hills, and in 1996, won a *Sydney Morning Herald Good Food Guide* chef's hat. He went to the award ceremony, but didn't collect his.

Jennifer and I went dressed to the hilt – I hired a suit,
I didn't own one. Everyone was there, [chef] Neil
Perry ... [SMH reviewer] Terry Durack was there.
He turned up scruffy as. It infuriated me. I can't
believe I went out of my way to look decent and he
looked like he'd just turned up from the office.
I thought, fuck it, I don't need it. The next year we
put a sign in the window saying 'This restaurant
chooses not to be reviewed by the *Good Food
Guide*.' I got a call from Mr Durack saying 'It's not
your choice' and I said, 'I'm afraid it is.' I sold the
restaurant before the *Good Food Guide* came out and
went overseas.

He went to Paris and cooked in two restaurants,
Bennelong and Woolloomooloo, in the second of
which he had a financial stake. But money problems
intervened, and he came back to Australia. In talking
about what he had done, he says, 'I was certain that this
was the advancement of the Australian cuisine – but I
could never get past this fucking bush tucker thing.'
But he recognises the part that he played, with just a
touch of regret. 'I'm not getting the recognition for it,
but at least it's out there. People like Kylie Kwong and
[Sydney chef] Chris Manfield and Clayton Donovan
have taken it up. That's fine. I started something.' And
what he started, he called Australian cuisine. Of the
ingredients he pioneered he said:

They're unique ingredients. What's important is not that they're Aboriginal, but that they're flavours and components that can turn into cuisine. The Asians have done it with all their ingredients. Why can't we? And let's make things like the wonga pigeon and the magpie goose special, not everyday food.

I knew I was onto something and I wanted the press to understand this was a development of Australian cuisine. I didn't invent it, but if we want to develop it this was the way to go. If you're in Germany and I put a German meal in front of you, a Thai meal in Thailand, a French meal in France, [along with] an Australian meal, it will stand on its own because it is different in flavour to the others. It has these additional flavours incorporated into it from the ingredients grown here. Then along came Raymond Kersh and Andrew Fielke.

Bruneteau is back in Australia, but no longer cooking. At the time of writing, he was happily driving a bus on the north shore. He's happy, but I'm sad that the creativity of this man is not being tapped for young cooks. Little respect is given to our pioneers.

But if this pioneer was French, following hot on his heels were a couple of dinky di Australians from Pyrmont, which, at the time of their growing up, was, as Ruth Park wrote in her splendid book *The Companion Guide to Sydney*, 'as seductive as a boilermaker's yard'.

Brother and sister Jennice and Raymond Kersh are

an unlikely pair in almost every respect. Unlikely to have come out of Pyrmont, where their father Abe was, as described by Jennice, Sydney's only Jewish wharf labourer. And unlikely to become ardent supporters of cooking with native ingredients. Chef Raymond is an unlikely chef, in that his first choice of professions was couturier: he still designs and makes all his own clothes. He's also dyslexic and has never read a cookbook. So how did it happen?

For a start, Abe was, as well as a wharf labourer, a man 'with an incredible talent for food' .They ate very well in Pyrmont. Mother Edna was also a fine, if more conventional, cook, whose hospitality gave rise to the names of their three restaurants, Edna's Table I, II and III. Raymond sidled into cooking, almost by accident, and Jennice – who really should have been an actress – became the animateur for the restaurants, which were as much about theatre as they were about food. The floor was Jennice's stage.

The native food component came about from a holiday with their brother John in Balgo in the Kimberley, where he had established a cattle station for the mission. Although Raymond had eaten and cooked kangaroo, wallaby, emu and crocodile, and cooked with native limes on Dunk Island, it was their exposure to, and friendship with, the Kukatja people at Balgo that completed their conversion. They 'introduced us to native bush food, and their strong distinctive flavours were like nothing we'd ever had before.'

In 1981, they opened the first Edna's Table in Kent Street. It bamboozled the critics (the *Good Food Guide* classed it as 'Eclectic') and delighted its patrons. Having been to Balgo and been introduced to the flavours of Australia, Raymond did introduce some native ingredients:

> But not any meats at the time – bush tomato and native thyme and pepperberries. They weren't so much hard to get as they were expensive. And that's why it was hard. And you couldn't put on the menu what you were using, because nobody knew what they were anyway – we were just using them to create flavours, but not specify[ing] what we were using.

Edna's Table II at the MLC Centre was where the Kershes came out of the culinary closet. The restaurant was an Indigenously themed extravaganza, not only on the menu but in the décor that had the critics pursing their lips. An early (1996) review suggested that 'the marriage of native flavours and contemporary technique sometimes feels like cultural imperialism ... the heavily themed décor (boomerang-backed chairs) can get a bit much.' Sydney at least didn't seem ready for this new Australian cuisine.

Putting the ingredients on the menu 'scared the living daylights out of the customers,' Jennice said. It was, Raymond now admits, 'the worst move we ever made. Before, we were using it and people were eating it unaware.' Just how bad the reaction was is revealed in a story told me by Raymond:

> We had a customer who was a real regular. He was a fantastic customer. He came to the MLC and ate the same food [he'd been eating at Kent Street] and read on the menu what he'd been eating all along and he turned around and said to me, 'What are you using this Abo shit for?'

That wasn't an isolated instance. 'The resistance and the judgement on what we were doing absolutely blew us away,' Jennice said. 'We couldn't believe it. It hurt. And we talked about it and said – what must it feel [like] to be Aboriginal?' She went on to say:

> We believed in it. Every cuisine in the world has been created from the food of the land – and we couldn't use the food of Australia. We were putting up with this unbelievable rejection. People would stop me in the street and say 'Jennice, I used to love your restaurant, but you're doing all that bush tucker. I'm sorry.'

'It wasn't just the customers,' Raymond said. 'It was other chefs as well.' Jennice said, 'The inaugural Restaurant & Catering Awards we won the first two years for Best Modern Australian restaurant in Sydney. One particular chef came up and scoffed at it to my face.'

But they pushed on and in 1999 opened a more conventionally decorated restaurant – although Indigenous art adorned the walls – in Clarence Street, without changing the emphasis on the menu. The critics were kinder, but still somewhat patronising, as in 'the effort to domesticate Australian ingredients is heroic.' This last Edna's Table closed in 2005. 'Business came in spurts,' said Raymond. 'You're flavour of the month one week, then nothing.' Closing was, Jennice said, 'heartbreaking. We were losing money. And when you have an upmarket restaurant, you lose big. The overheads were enormous.'

I asked Raymond Kersh why they thought Australians have rejected native produce for so long. 'Convict complex. Jennice and I suffer from Pyrmont peasant complex; I think the whole country suffers from convict complex. You're still a servant to England.' Let's hope that's changed.

The third of the first wave native Australian food chefs, Andrew Fielke, is not from Sydney. He began as a chef, originally at his Red Ochre restaurants, and is now a grower and supplier, TV chef and educator. He was the inaugural chair of the peak industry body Australian Native Food Industry Limited (ANFIL). He grew up in Renmark on the Murray river, and it was there that he first began to think about the food that grew around him.

I remember playing marbles with quandong stones
as a kid growing up on the Murray, because they're
beautiful round stones. It struck me then and there
that we never cooked quandong pie, Mum never
made quandong jam and they grew all around the
area. Why the hell didn't we use this marvellous
fruit? So I started learning a lot more through the
likes of people like Vic Cherikoff. That's been my
career ever since, specialising in native foods.

Fielke opened the first Red Ochre restaurant in
Adelaide in 1992 – there are now three, all independ-
ent, two in Adelaide and one in Alice Springs, none
owned by Fielke. He sold the Adelaide restaurant in
2001 and began working internationally as a guest chef.

I wanted to take native foods to a much wider
audience than just one restaurant. So I started with
food service products, because that was a much
cheaper option than the expensive packaging
associated with consumer products and I thought I
could use my contacts. So I started by selling raw
native ingredients and then began to value-add them
and that has been my business for the last twelve
or thirteen years. It has been great for me, I've seen
fantastic growth in the last few years. There are more
growers, some fresh stuff coming onto the market.
And a lot of the chefs want it now, chefs like Neil
Perry – I saw native thyme and muntries on his

menu. Kylie Kwong has been using a lot and even at Quay they're using native ingredients from time to time.

Fielke has stuck with native foods through the difficult times.

I was beating my head against a brick wall for years and years. I think people were too reserved, the old bush tucker stigma, it was seen as outback, crass, ocker – that was one thing. I don't think too many chefs had the foresight to look at the true regional food in Australia, they've only looked at introduced regional food. And that is a real shame, I've despaired at it many, many times – why haven't more chefs taken it on? Why haven't they been blown away by the flavours, as I have?

It would appear that many chefs today are being 'blown away by the flavours', but using them in different ways. Prominent among what I call the converts is Peter Gilmore, executive chef at Quay restaurant in Sydney, and one of Australia's most awarded chefs. For fourteen consecutive years. Quay has been awarded three chefs hats in *The Sydney Morning Herald Good Food Guide* and it has been named Restaurant of the Year six times. He describes his food as 'inspired by nature' and has an extensive experimental garden in his home. It was a home-grown tree that got him started. 'René

[Redzepi] was part of the catalyst for that change,' Gilmore told me, 'but I was going through the process at around the same time.'

> One of the things that happened to me, about four years ago I moved into this place that had all these lilly pilly trees in the backyard and I remember reading something in Gay Bilson's book *Plenty* about a lilly pilly jam. When I moved into this house they were all ripe on the tree, and I tasted them and I thought, wow, they are really, really cool and quite exciting, and so I started experimenting with some sugar and some vanilla and I realised this was a really wonderful native fruit and so underutilised.

Having read this far, you'll be struck by the irony of Gilmore inventing the wheel once again. What he was doing is what Bruneteau had done in the early 1980s. But Gilmore went further. While the early chefs had to put up with either second-rate or dried or frozen produce, by the time he was sitting up and taking notice, there were producers who could supply what he wanted.

Having 'discovered' the lilly pilly (or riberry), as a chef interested in fresh and natural ingredients, Gilmore began to wonder about it. What were its seasons around the country, and could he get supplies of fresh fruit? With the now available wonder of the internet, he did a search and came up with Outback Pride. 'I rang them up and spoke to Gayle and Mike Quarmby. I said to Mike, "Can you get me lilly pillies?" and he said, "Yeah, they're frozen." And I said, "No, I want fresh ones.'"

Quarmby replied that they were in season on his property as they spoke, and he could send some to him, no problem. It was just that no one had ever asked for fresh fruit before. Gilmore continues the story:

> They came up to Sydney and we had a meeting, that was about four years ago, and they sat down and put this incredible array of native fruit and herbs in front of me and all were frozen or dried. For me, when you freeze something you lose a lot of its intensity and a lot of its character, and when you dry it you intensify it and it's overpowering. And I said, "Can we get hold of some of this stuff fresh?" That started a new direction for them. They started thinking about getting things fresh for chefs. They visited Kylie Kwong and I recommended a couple of chefs, so we started buying fresh things off them, muntries, when they're in season. We have them on the menu in February/March for about six weeks, beautiful little miniature fruit like apples. We put them in a little salad and people go, 'Wow, what are these things?' No one's ever had them in a restaurant fresh before – they're always frozen or in a jam. That's the difference.

But that's not the only difference. Gilmore doesn't trumpet his use of native flora; doesn't make a fuss of it. It's just another set of ingredients. When we look at our most interesting Australian chefs – and Gilmore is certainly one of those – we see that they are appropriating not just European but Asian, Middle Eastern, Indian, Mexican, etc., ingredients and techniques, weaving together ingredients and techniques from more than one cuisine in a manner that could be described as bricolage.

Bricolage is the right term for cuisines like Gilmore's, what is called Modern Australian. It is used to signify the creation of a work or works from a diverse range of materials at hand. The anthropologist and ethnologist Lévi-Strauss borrowed the word from one of its modern (French language) uses, meaning do-it-yourself projects around the house. Bricolage, in Lévi-Strauss's sense, was an attempt to re-use available materials in order to solve new problems. Thus the Modern Australian chef casts about for ingredients and techniques which can be used in ways that they would not have been used in their original context to create a dish never before seen and, in most instances, never to be seen again. In this instance, native flora. But Gilmore says:

You don't want it to become a huge, blown-up thing. [You want] all those ingredients in their own right and incorporated into the modern Australian cuisine in a gentle and thoughtful sort of way if it works, not [to] throw things together because they're native. If a little bit of native purslane works within a dish where I have other ingredients, it's just a beautiful ingredient that gives some character within that dish. And the dish works in the context of modern Australian cooking. It's not to make it gimmicky, it's to incorporate it as a natural seamless ingredient into the cuisine we're developing in Australia, which is multicultural Australian food. On its own merit, not because it is native, but on its merit. That's what's really cool about how we're using it now.

That's a sentiment echoed by 28-year-old chef Matt Stone, who was first exposed to native ingredients at his first restaurant, Star Anise in Perth. A local supplier dropped off some samples.

We looked at them and we never really used them. The head chef wasn't really interested. I was pretty keen, I was sous chef at the time. Most of the ingredients came frozen, so that deterred him. I really enjoyed them. Then, when I was the head chef at the Greenhouse and I had the chance to do what I liked, I got in contact with the supplier again and started using some native fruits and spices, and progressed from there. That would have been 2009/10.

But, like Gilmore, Stone puts them in their place. 'If you crap on about it, it makes it a bit gimmicky. I've just integrated them into my food and just treated them as I would any other ingredient.'

Like most of the converts, he was influenced by Noma and also D.O.M. in São Paulo.

Places that built their cuisine from their surroundings – that was the big push at the start. And then once I discovered them and I began enjoying the flavours and recognising the health benefits and the localism, it has become a real driving force in my cooking.

This chapter began and will now end with Indigenous chefs. Firstly, the multi-talented Mark 'Black' Olive: chef, caterer, film writer and producer, educator and ambassador for Indigenous Australia. Olive is also a pioneer, having been cooking for thirty-six years.

I did my apprenticeship [in Wollongong] in the '70s and early '80s, after watching my aunt and mother cooking, and going back to the mission in Bundjalung country. My parents were from up there and my family's still up there. We used to travel back every year. There was lots of wattleseed and lemon myrtle – it's the home of the aniseed myrtle and lemon myrtle. We experimented with lots of food back then.

He began his apprenticeship in a local restaurant, but when that restaurant went under, he transferred to what was then called Wollongong Hospital.

Everyone said, you did your apprenticeship in a hospital? But what they forget is back then, everything was fresh, not this frozen stuff that's sent out now. Back then every day there was a new beginning. Not only that, we got to rotate around in the kitchen as well. One day I'd be on sweets, then meats, then breakfasts. We had diabetes and kidney disease in our family and when I got into the dietary kitchen I learnt how to maintain kidney health.

The other aspect of working in a large hospital and serving up to 1000 meals a day was that 'you get your skills up. Later, when cooking for Tourism Australia, a dinner for 2000 did not faze me.'

In 1993, he moved to Sydney, studied film at the Australian Film Television and Radio School, and opened a restaurant, Midden, in Pitt Street. Then to Melbourne, where he opened a catering company, and did a BA in production and directing at the Victorian College of the Arts.

That's where I wrote *Outback Cafe*, over three years while I was at school. I graduated in 2003, and was approached to put together the series. Foxtel picked it up and it's been shown in over 100 countries.

My focus is to get more Aboriginal people out there. And then Clayton came along and now he's got his TV show. I first showcased bush food on TV in 1999 or 2000. It sparked interest in Aboriginal food, which was great. During all that time I've been involved with the growers, making products. Its been very diverse, very stressful. I've been ripped off three times really badly, but you know you've just got to get back onto the horse and keep going. I think if we can showcase what we've done to Aboriginal kids coming through hospitality, I hope they think there is opportunity, there is scope, and you can fly as high as you want.

And that is what he's doing. Training young Aboriginal children in hospitality.

I had a group in Bunbury and Echuca and from twenty we've been able to get five into apprenticeships, which has been great. Now we're looking for the next group. It all comes down to money. It's interesting that even today people think Aboriginal issues aren't important; not only that, but that the product isn't viable. Yet here we have this amazing food source in Australia. We've embraced every other culture except what we've got here. What we have here is unique; it's our national cuisine.

Next, Olive's friend and (one-time) neighbour Clayton Donovan. Donovan grew up on Gumbaynggirr and Bundjalung country on the mid north coast of New South Wales. When I first met him, he had a successful restaurant at Nambucca Heads, Jaaning Tree. The plaque in the restaurant told customers that:

> Our name, Jaaning pronounced 'jaa-nee', is
> Gumbaynggirr for the *Acacia irrorata* or Wattle tree. For
> centuries this tree has been a unique source of food
> for the local indigenous people. The new tree stems
> are rolled in the thick sweet sap that oozes from the
> bark to make 'bush lollies'. The tree is also unique in its
> ability to flower when all other wattles have finished.

Donovan closed the restaurant to take advantage of an offer to star in his own television show, *Wild Kitchen*, the first series of which ran for eleven episodes in 2014 on ABC television. A second series is under consideration as I write.

Donovan grew up in Macksville and Scotts Head. At high school there, although he wanted to, he wasn't allowed to do home science, which translates as cooking. 'It was the best place to be, in the kitchen with heaps of girls and loads of food. I had to do metal work. But I always did casual jobs in kitchens.' His family all cooked – his mother very well – and his best friend was an Italian. As he said, he had his mother's culinary tourism at home and his friend's Italian food. And he had an aunt who took him foraging.

> When I was about four or five my aunty Jess picked
> me up and took me out and showed me bush foods
> at Nambucca Heads. We'd go out and find jaaning
> – she had a bit of a sweet tooth and we'd go out and
> collect the sap off the wattle trees. She showed me
> bush carrots and parsnips, plants that healed, herbs.
> Every time we'd get ready to go and see Aunty Jess
> we'd go and collect things for her. Obviously I was
> too young to remember it all, but she planted this
> monster in the back of my head.

I asked Donovan about the herbs, how they were
used. It led to a discussion of the family's food.

> When my grandparents got native pipis they'd make
> pipi fritters with the native carrots. But the other
> stuff, they'd just eat them. There are no Australian
> native recipes – no structured sense of creating a
> dish. The food was there: eat it. But [my mother
> and grandparents] would make bolognese and use
> kangaroo mince – stuff like that. And my [paternal]
> family up in Cairns – Dad's sister Aunty Val works for
> the church. She incorporated a lot of Indonesian and
> PNG food – flying fox stew, for example – it's a really
> good sweet meat. An amalgamation of PNG, and
> Indonesian. Only there and in Broome have I seen
> those kinds of dishes.

At eighteen, Donovan wanted to play football. He played for Ballina and got a scholarship to play for Cronulla. But he broke his back. 'I wanted to box, I wanted to play footy and I wanted to be a chef. I told the doctor and he said, "You'll never be a chef." That's what kicked me on.'

He played in a band in Newcastle, went to law school in Lismore. 'I didn't like it. I remember my grandfather – who just passed – saying to me, "Do something that makes you happy every day." So I got back into the kitchen and went down to Sydney.'

He started knocking on doors and came across Kenneth Leung, 'who was using bush foods. He began using pipis, wattleseeds, myrtle and kangaroo, and amalgamated it with his food from all around the world. This was in the mid '90s.'

More kitchens, and marriage to his English wife Jane, led him to Cornwall and then back to Sydney to open Jaaning Tree in 1999. I told him of Watkin Tench's observation, in talking about the flavour of a native fruit, that 'were it meliorated by cultivation, it would become more palatable' and asked him why there'd been so little communication, from both sides, about the food of the land. 'I don't know why,' he said. 'Blatant ignorance on both sides? There was a period of time when I was growing up when knowledge would not be passed on – and it wouldn't be passed on to a white person.' Why was that?

They'd be scared to tell you. It would have been lack of trust. Knowledge is power. Would they give it to the new settlers to farm? In hindsight, it would have been great for our people ... ignorance on one side, and mistrust on the other – women were being raped, there were massacres, they would have been scared. It has to change. Now with the idea of sustainability and the rest of the world falling in love with our native foods, we might decide we love them, if you put them in a space where people can understand them better. For example, I've got some really good scallops and I do a coconut water foam and a quandong and native peach reduction around the bottom, and if they ask they'll find out what they're eating. After four years I've got people coming back and saying they've found a quandong plant and they're growing it at home – what can they do with the fruit?

He recalls when he first opened the restaurant, 'a friend called Dennis said, "I've been waiting for you." He and his wife grow native foods. Once it gets into the cultivation stage, it'll snowball.' ('Dennis' was Dennis Ryan of Valley of the Mists – see the Appendix, 'A list of Australian edible plants, animals and grains'.)

Peter Gilmore talked about using native produce 'on its own merit, not because it is native, but on its merit. That's what really cool about how we're using it now.' Is it really cool? Do we have to bury these ingredients surreptitiously in dishes in order for them to be accepted? If you asked Raymond Kersh, he would say 'Of course'. Revealing the ingredients he'd been using was, he said, 'the worst move we ever made'. And while Gilmore is not exactly hiding the ingredients, and admires and respects them, in his menu, as he says, he's going to 'incorporate them into the modern Australian cuisine in a gentle and thoughtful sort of way'. Either this is a shame, or it's the way we can get over the resistance.

The other possibility is that a dual market develops. On the one hand, native ingredients will be highlighted on television, on shows like *Outback Cafe* and *Wild Kitchen*, to encourage export sales and tourism. And at home, chefs simply use them as another set of ingredients. In that way, their use will trickle down over time from the professional kitchen to the home kitchen, as so many ingredients have. That trickle-down effect is now a marketing strategy: sell the ingredient to the high-end restaurant kitchen, and then gradually let it out to retail.

At the risk of turning this book into a marketing manual, I have a suggestion for the industry. Recently, I went looking for Paroo Kangaroo (see chapter 7, 'The producers'). And I wanted to cook it with a sauce that used mountain pepper. The retailer listed as stocking Paroo fillets did not have them. I returned three times and gave up. On my first trip there, I also searched through their extensive spice racks for mountain pepper. There was none.

If they are to persuade Australians to eat native foods, producers must at least ensure they are stocked, and that complementary ingredients are stocked, preferably close at hand. This is the ex-advertising man talking.

Will these ingredients trickle down from the professional to the home kitchen? As more and more of them appear on the menus of admired chefs, and if past behaviour is any guide, they should. As long as they can be found!

PETER GILMORE

CHARCOAL-GRILLED MARRON, NATIVE COASTAL GREENS AND LEMON ASPEN

Serves 8

Native coastal greens and lemon aspen
100 g barilla (Coorong spinach)
150 g karkalla (sea succulent)
100 g munyeroo (native purslane)
50 g sea parsley (sea celery)
32 fresh lemon aspen fruits

Seaweed dressing
1 small eschallot, finely diced
sea salt flakes

2 sheets of Korean toasted nori
100 ml grape seed oil
1 tsp lemon juice
8 marron, 250 g each
melted clarified butter
sea salt flakes

1. Pick through the barilla, karkalla, munyeroo and sea
    parsley, keeping only the small tips and leaves. Discard
    any larger leaves and stems. Wash well, drain and set
    aside until required.

2. Pick and remove any stems from the lemon aspen fruit,
    then set fruit aside until required.

3. To make the seaweed dressing, put the eschallot in a
    mortar with a good pinch of sea salt flakes and crush
    with a pestle until a paste is formed. Roughly chop
    the nori, add to the mortar with a small amount of
    the grapeseed oil and combine until a rough paste is
    formed. Drizzle in the remaining oil and lemon juice and
    combine well.

4. To prepare the marron for cooking, first place them
    in plenty of iced water and leave for a minimum of
    15 minutes to humanely despatch them. Bring a large
    saucepan of salted water to the boil. Blanch the marron
    for one minute, then return to the iced water: this will
    help in extracting the meat from the shell.

5. Use a large kitchen knife to cut the head from the
    marron. Use kitchen scissors to cut along both sides of
    the softer underside shell. Peel the underside back and

then use your fingers to carefully pull the tail meat from the shell, keeping the skin intact.

6. Remove the fine film of skin from the belly of the marron then score one cut down the centre of the belly – being careful not to cut all the way through – then open out the flesh. Set aside in the fridge until required.

7. To cook the marron, brush them liberally with grapeseed oil and season well with sea salt flakes. Put the marron on the grill, skin-side down. Allow the heat to slightly roast the skin for 1–2 minutes. Turn the marron over and finish cooking (2–3 minutes). Remove marron from the grill, brush with melted clarified butter and allow to rest for 1 minute.

8. Meanwhile, blanch the coastal greens in salted boiling water for 30 seconds. Drain, brush with melted butter and season with sea salt flakes. Gently warm the lemon aspen fruit in a small saucepan with a small amount of melted clarified butter and sea salt.

9. To plate, place a marron in the centre of each warmed serving plate. Dab a few dots of the seaweed dressing around the marron. Garnish the marron with the warmed lemon aspen and coastal greens and serve.

Peter Gilmore is the executive chef at Quay and Bennelong. Quay has been in the list of the Top Fifty Restaurants in the World since 2009. Peter is a recent convert to Australian native produce. This recipe is from Peter Gilmore, *Organum: Nature, Texture, Intensity, Purity*, Murdoch Books, 2014, p. 207. Reproduced by permission of Allen & Unwin Pty Ltd.

CHRIS JACKMAN

....

COLD SCALLOP RAVIOLI WITH BRAISED LETTUCE

Serves 6

400 g Triabunna (on the east coast of Tasmania) scallops
500 ml fish stock
lime leaves, fresh or frozen
1 stick fresh lemongrass, sliced
1 red chilli, cut in half, seeds removed, then finely diced
1½ green chillies, cut in half, seeds removed, then finely
    diced
⅓ of a fresh coconut, flesh grated
1 tbsp light soy sauce
½ tbsp safflower oil
24 won ton wrappers
coriander sprigs
white of 1 egg, lightly beaten
½ iceberg lettuce, blanched in fish stock, then cooled

Dressing
½ red chilli, seeded and finely diced
1 green chilli, seeded and finely diced
30 ml fish sauce
200 ml water
100 ml lemon juice

1. To make the dressing, mix all the ingredients together. Dress the cold lettuce with the dressing, and keep cool until required.
2. Blanch the scallops in fish stock, together with 2 or 3 lime leaves and scraps left over from slicing the lemongrass. When cool, mix the scallops with the sliced lemongrass, red chilli, green chilli, grated coconut flesh, light soy sauce and safflower oil.
3. Lay 12 won ton wrappers out on a bench. Place a coriander sprig on each (not too close to the edge). On top of these place another won ton wrapper, sandwiching the coriander. Pass through a pasta machine at number 6, turn around and pass through again to form a square.
4. Brush 6 of the squares with a little egg white and place a neat even pile of the scallop mix into the centre of each. Leave a 10 cm border free of the mixture, so the edges of the wrappers will stick together. Lay the other wrappers on top. Press gently to remove air and seal the edges with your fingertips.
5. Blanch each raviolo separately for 15 seconds on each side using a spider (or large slotted spoon) to remove from the pot. Refresh in a bowl of cold water.
6. To serve, place a raviolo in the centre of each plate. Arrange the lettuce around the edge of the ravioli, together with sprigs of coriander.

Chris Jackman was a Tasmanian-born Indigenous chef. His restaurant, Mit Zitrone, was one of the most influential in Hobart. Chris died in 2012.

11

WALKING TOGETHER,
EATING TOGETHER

Syzygium anisatum

Having said sorry, we refuse to say thanks.

Bruce Pascoe

On the last Thursday of November every year, Americans of all ethnic backgrounds, colours and religions gather in their family homes to eat a ritual meal, comprising a mix of Native American, European and, latterly, ingredients from their own food cultures. This is a feast whose roots can possibly be found in an expression of joy at bringing in the first harvest in a new land, but which has transformed into a celebration of the idea of America.

I write 'possibly' because there are arguments

among historians about the term 'thanksgiving'. They need not concern us here. What is relevant to us is the food on the table and the people around it at the celebratory meal in 1621. Here's how it happened.

On 16 September 1620, 102 passengers seeking religious freedom set off from Plymouth, Devon. They arrived at the mouth of the Hudson River on 6 November, after a difficult and uncomfortable journey, and at what is now Plymouth in Massachusetts in December. After a terrible winter, they planted their first crops in the spring of 1621.

'On March 16', James W. Baker wrote in *Thanksgiving: The Biography of an American Holiday*, 'a lone Indian entered the settlement and astonished the colonists by greeting them in English. This was Samoset, a Native Sagamore from Maine.' Samoset introduced them to Squanto, who also spoke English and who was to become the colony's translator and instructor in the planting of corn and other local resources. In autumn, 'the all-important corn harvest that would insure Plymouth Colony's survival proved successful, although some of the English crops were a disappointment.'

The claim for a first thanksgiving in 1621 to celebrate that crop was not made until 1841 by Alexander Young, author of the *Chronicles of the Pilgrim Fathers of the Colony of Plymouth*. In that book he published a letter from the pilgrim (and later third governor) Edward Winslow, dated 11 December 1621. Originally published in England in the hope of attracting settlers, the letter was promptly forgotten, only to be redis-covered in the 1820s. It described a three-day event at the Plymouth Plantation, the dates of which were not given. Winslow wrote:

> Our harvest being gotten in, our Governor sent
> four men on fowling, that so we might after a
> more special manner rejoice together, after we had
> gathered the fruit of our labours. They four in one
> day killed as much fowl as, with a little help besides,
> served the Company almost a week. At which
> time, amongst other recreations, we exercised our
> arms, many of the Indians coming amongst us, and
> amongst the rest their greatest king, Massasoit, with
> some 90 men, whom for three days we entertained
> and feasted. And they went out and killed five deer
> which they brought to the plantation and bestowed
> on our Governor and upon the Captain and others.

In a footnote to Winslow's letter, Young claims this as the first Thanksgiving, offering as support Governor William Bradford's report that in the fall of 1621 the settlers had accumulated 'a great store of wild turkeys, venison, cod, bass, waterfowl and corn'.

At the centre of this national feast was, and is, the turkey. In her chapter 'The invention of Thanksgiving: a ritual of American nationality' in Carole M. Couni-han's *Food in the USA: A Reader*, Janet Siskind says that 'more than just a part of the wilderness that had been civilized, the thanksgiving turkey powerfully symbol-izes the Indians.'

A native animal at the centre of a ritual feast that defines Americans as Americans. Other native foods at the table were – and still are – pumpkins and cranber-ries (recipes for which appeared in the first American cookbook, *American Cookery* by Amelia Simmons, pub-lished in 1796) and barberries.

There are parallels and there are striking differ-ences, the most obvious of which is that America was founded on the idea of liberty, and Australia as a penal colony. Another obvious difference was between Native Americans and the Indigenous people encoun-tered by the British here: the Native Americans had recognisable farm crops and were clothed.

But at the heart of this narrative is the story of first contact, a story which involves co-operation, accept-ance of native foods, a shared meal and, eventually, the emergence of one item from that table as a symbol of both the Indigenous and the idea of America. If you have read this book up to here, you won't need to be reminded of the contrast between these first contacts. But let us examine the Australian version of first con-tact a little more closely.

Governor Arthur Phillip had orders from King George III to 'endeavour, by every possible means, to open an intercourse with the natives, and to con-ciliate their affections, enjoining all subjects to live in amity and kindness with them'. Unfortunately, the locals wanted nothing to do with these newcomers, and stayed away from them after February 1788. This so frustrated Phillip that he kidnapped a local called Arabanoo by subterfuge.

Two boats were sent to Manly Cove, where, according to Watkin Tench, 'several Indians were seen standing on the beach.' They were enticed by 'courteous behaviour and a few presents to enter into conversation'. The presents were most likely the beads and red baize that were given to the people at Botany Bay, where the fleet landed briefly. Once the group approached 'our soldiers rushed in amongst them and seized two men.' But only one, Arabanoo, was secured.

He was fastened by ropes to the boat, where he 'set up the most piercing and lamentable cries of distress'. After being offered some fish he 'sullenly submitted to his destiny'. Which was to be taken by force to the governor's residence.

As we have since learnt, the Indigenous inhabitants had extraordinary methods of communication and doubtless stories like Phillip's capture and chaining of Arabanoo, although the man came to no harm, would have been alarming. This was not how guests behaved with their hosts.

There was a meal. The captured man was taken to a side table at the governor's residence – not the main table – and according to Tench 'ate heartily of fish and ducks which he first cooled'. He smelled at the bread and salt meat but wouldn't eat it, and would drink nothing but water, disdaining the 'liquors' offered him.

He was careful with his table manners, having closely watched others eating, and only made two mistakes: wiping his hands on his chair, and throwing his plate out the window as he would have a leaf or a piece of bark.

We know that relations with Native Americans deteriorated rapidly, as did those with the Indigenous inhabitants of Australia. But those contrasting stories of first contact are revealing: one a meal of celebration, and one where the guest had been kidnapped. The relationship did not begin with trust; certainly not with celebration. European Australians have a lot of bridges to build to restore relations with their Indigenous neighbours.

At the head of this chapter I quote Bruce Pascoe: 'Having said sorry, we refuse to say thanks.' And there is the germ of an idea.

In writing this book I came across one author, Laklak Burarrwanga (she also credits her family), whose book *Welcome to My Country*, although sold as a children's book, is a book for all ages. In it she tells the story of the life she and her family live in north-east Arnhem land. Laklak is of the Yolnu (often spelt Yolngu) people. At the end of the book, she writes: 'When my grandmothers collected food, they saved it in a basket and shared it. Now we are putting our knowledge in a basket and we share it – mother to grandchildren – and now you have to share it with your family.'

I am attempting, with this book, to share the food that non-Indigenous Australians have turned their backs on for so many years. And here, at the end, I would like to make a proposal.

Australia Day on 26 January celebrates the day Captain Phillip raised the English flag at Sydney Cove. It continues to be a contentious day; some even call it Invasion Day.

I would like to suggest that we celebrate the day, in our cities and towns, with a meal of native Australian foods shared between European and Aboriginal Australians. To take up Pascoe's suggestion, the meal would be giving thanks to the Indigenous inhabitants for caring for the country, and – admittedly belatedly – showing us the foods of the land.

How this would be achieved and who would organise it would need to be carefully worked out. The obvious organisers would be the various Australia Day Committees, in conjunction with ANFIL. But this would, I believe, entirely change the meaning of Australia Day. We might even change the name. But one thing at a time – first, sharing a meal. It's never too late.

As I wrote in the introduction, 'non-Indigenous Australians must accept that the original inhabitants have carefully stewarded this land for the entire time they have lived here, and have the oldest unbroken culture in the world, before that racism – culinary and otherwise – will disappear.' At the end of *The Biggest Estate on Earth*, Bill Gammage writes: 'We have a continent to learn. If we are to survive, let alone feel at home, we must begin to understand our country. If we succeed, one day we might become Australian.'

One way of achieving this may well be to sit down as brothers and sisters and share a meal.

MATT STONE

....

CRISPY CRICKETS, MILL WORMS, AUSSIE 7 SPICE

I truly believe that bugs have a big hand in a sustainable food future. In Asia and South America it's completely normal to eat bugs on a daily basis. They're full of protein and high in vitamin K2. They take only a few weeks to grow to full size and can be grown in small spaces – they don't need huge paddocks. They can be completely raised on our food waste. It's a long process to get the average Aussie eating them, so starting off with a salty, spicy snack with a drink is a great way to introduce eating bugs.

50 g crickets
30 g mill worms
½ tsp 7 spice
salt to taste
fermented chilli sauce
wild herbs

1. The Aussie 7 spice can be made ahead of time. See p. 43 for the recipe.
2. The bugs will more than likely be frozen, so be sure to take them out of the freezer a few hours before cooking.
3. Heat some cottonseed oil in a fryer or pot to 180°C. *Slowly and carefully* place the bugs in, making sure the oil doesn't boil over. Stir often and cook for 3–4 minutes, until golden and crisp.
4. Remove the bugs from the oil and drain well. Mix with the 7 spice and season with salt to taste. Place in a small bowl. Add a few random dots of fermented chilli sauce and finish with some wild herbs for a little freshness, for example crushed lemon myrtle leaves, mountain pepper leaf or native thyme. Wood sorrel is great, as it adds a zingy, sour note. Serve immediately.

APPENDIX
A LIST OF AUSTRALIAN EDIBLE PLANTS, ANIMALS AND GRAINS

The wild food forager should always exercise care
and consideration. Fruits are the foods of birds
and mammals, so some of each crop should be left
untouched. Soil upturned by digging for tubers can
create habitat for introduced weeds. Aborigines were
sometimes wasteful, but we cannot afford to be –
there is too little wilderness left.

Tim Low

Below is a list of the native foods that have emerged as
the most used and the most popular in this third phase
of our engagement with them. It would be impossible
to list all the edible plants that grow here: Australian
science and agricultural writer Julian Cribb estimates
there are over 6000 plants with edible parts in Australia. Tim Low lists 180 of them in *Wild Food Plants of
Australia*.

To plant foods I have added animals, but not insects
and grubs: these will come, but it's the next step. The

grubs, for example, really do need to be eaten at source in spite of a tinned product, 'witchetty grub and bunya nut soup', mentioned in an article in *Meanjin* by Linda Soukoulis in 1990. (The grubs were 'simmered in chicken and vegetable stock' for ten minutes before being 'pureed through a sieve'.)

I have not listed those few native foods we have regularly eaten: the macadamia, yabbies, marron, barramundi and oysters for example (see the Introduction).

Some of the foods listed you can only buy in preparations; some you can grow yourself; others you will have to search for, either online or in the wild. If you do forage, remember, some wild food plants are poisonous. The records of the early explorers are littered with accounts of illness and even death from eating the wrong plants, or plants not properly prepared (often because the explorer didn't think to ask the locals how to do so). Indeed, according to Tim Low, the first Europeans known to have eaten wild foods here were the crew of the Dutch explorer Willem de Vlamingh in Western Australia in 1696. They ate raw cycad seeds, perhaps having seen the local people harvest them, and vomited violently.

A far more sensible approach was taken by Ludwig Leichhardt, as outlined in his journal. 'I frequently tasted the fine-looking fruit of the Pandanus,' he wrote, 'but was every time severely punished with sore lips and a blistered tongue; and the first time that I ate it, I was attacked by a violent diarrhoea.'

Observing vast heaps of pandanus in the Indigenous people's camps, he opined that it formed a good part of their diet, and set out to learn how they prepared it. He went on: 'I supposed that they washed out the sweet mealy matter contained between the stringy fibres, and that they drank the liquid, as they do with the honey; and that their large koolimans which we had occasionally seen, were used for the purpose.' Leichhardt followed the same procedure and, once processed, he found 'it lost almost all its sharpness, had a very pleasant taste, and, taken in moderate quantities, did not affect the bowels.' Finally he advises (from his own observations), 'The fruit should be so ripe as to be ready to drop from the tree.'

Not all fruit is eaten, for all manner of reasons; some is eaten by one group but not another, and much of what looks edible may not be. A general rule for foraging is that if a food is listed in a book of Indigenous foods as edible, then it is. But because of a greater variety of cooking methods – pots to boil in, for example – these foods can be treated in different ways. As you have seen, throughout the book there are recipes from chefs who have discovered, adapted and used these ingredients in their personal cuisines.

Among the foods listed are those that I and others in the native foods industry would like to see be made more available, and others that are being developed.

In the bibliography, you'll find a link to *The New Crop Industries Handbook: Native Food*, a very useful Rural

Industries Research and Development Corporation publication which will reward those who want more information on native fruits.

Finally, you'll find sources for many of these foods in the next section, 'Useful contacts', along with the websites of the Indigenous groups I have written about.

NATIVE FRUITS

DESERT LIME	
Botanical name	*Citrus glauca*
Description	The Australian desert lime fruit is round, small and green, with a lighter shade of green/yellow spots covering it. Once cut, the flesh inside has the same spots, with a bubble-like appearance.
	The plant is a shrub or small tree with blue-grey leaves, the lower branches covered in prickles and the higher branches, above 2 m, free from them. Flower-to-fruiting time is short, only 10–12 weeks. The plants mainly flower in spring so that the fruit is ripening by summer.
	The plants will usually be found growing in clumps on heavy clay soils. The desert lime is incredibly drought tolerant and can continue to thrive in heats of 45°C. It has the same level of tolerance to cold.
Location	South-west Queensland, western New South Wales and South Australia
Flavour	Like other citrus fruit, the desert lime flavour is tart, with astringency and bitterness. The aroma has been likened to brown lime citrus. The flavour is more intense than, say, the Tahitian lime. It was used as a thirst quencher by stockmen.
Health benefits	The desert lime is high in vitamins C and E, calcium, potassium and folate as well as lutein.
	It has exceptionally high levels of folate and vitamin C.
Uses	Excellent for marmalades and beverages, as well as candied peel. They need no peeling or preparation and freeze without loss of flavour or presentation characteristics when thawed.

Finger lime

Botanical name	*Citrus australasica*
Description	The finger lime is well named, its appearance being that of a short stubby green finger-like cylinder, up to 10 cm long. Its skin colouring can vary from a light speckled green, to yellow, brown, purple, red or a dark almost black green. The flesh inside also has variations of colour – green, yellow or pink. The flesh is noticeable for its tiny, slightly sticky 'bubbly' globules. It grows on a spiny tree, ranging from 3–10 m in height. The flower of the plant is small and white, and it has thick dark green leathery leaves. Other species – Garraway's, Russell River – are similar.
Location	Most commonly found along the Australian east coast, mainly from south-east Queensland to north-eastern New South Wales, in tropical to subtropical rainforest.
Flavour	The taste of the citrus is tart and tangy, and it has a very acidic pulp. Compared to other limes, its flavour is unique and the fruit is now highly prized.
Health benefits	High in vitamin C and potassium
Uses	Finger limes are best enjoyed raw and fresh. Cut the lime in half, then squeeze out the 'pearls' of the pulp from both halves. They are popularly used to complement seafood, melons and desserts. They also make excellent marmalade and jams. Delicious in a gin and tonic.

DAVIDSON PLUM

Botanical name	*Davidsonia jerseyana*, *Davidsonia pruriens*
Description	The predominant species cultivated is *D. jerseyana*. This species has the smallest tree. The fruit emerge from the trunk between November and February and look very much like Damson plums. Selections have been made for larger fruit, a leaf-free trunk and longer flower panicles. *D. pruriens* bears fruit in winter in its natural range; the fruiting period seems less clear in New South Wales. Fruit is borne on long flower panicles, generally from upper branches, but often from the tree trunk. The fruit is larger and paler than that of *D. jerseyana*.
Location	*D. jerseyana* is also called the New South Wales Davidson plum, and still grows, though rarely in the wild. *D. pruriens* is the predominant crop in Queensland, with much production in the past coming from the harvesting of naturally occurring trees.
Flavour	The aroma is of jam, fruity and earthy, like fresh beetroot. The fruit is extremely sour and tangy.
Health benefits	High in potassium, magnesium and manganese
Uses	Too sour to eat, but delicious and tangy when cooked. They make terrific jams, sauces, preserves and cordials, and work well in dairy products such as yogurt, and in sweets, wines and spirits. Versatile – equally good for sweet or savoury use.

Illawarra plum (brown pine)

Botanical name	Podocarpus elatus
Description	The tree on which the Illawarra plum grows, the brown pine, is tall and dense, with brown furrowed bark. It is unlike other rainforest trees in that it has tough, narrow and sharp-tipped leaves which are 2–8 cm long and 1 cm wide. The fruit grows in two segments, a hard external, inedible 1-cm-wide seed and the larger, edible purple-fleshed fruit.
Location	The Illawarra plum is native to and grows in subtropical eastern New South Wales and Queensland.
Flavour	The fruit is richly sweet, containing significant quantities of sticky sugars and has a plummy pine flavour. The core, however, is very resinous-tasting and best avoided.
Health benefits	The high level of sticky sugars is beneficial to the gastrointestinal tract. The antioxidant levels are seven times that of blueberries.
Uses	Primarily used for jams, conserves, desserts, sauces and beverages

KAKADU PLUM

Botanical name	*Terminalia ferdinandiana*
Description	The fruit is round and small, normally around 3 cm long and 1 cm wide, and contains a large seed. When ripened, the fruit is an olive yellow colour; it resembles a large, lumpy olive. The tree grows from small to medium-sized, is slender and has a grey-cream bark. Its leaves are a light green colour, arranged in clusters near the ends of the branches. Their shape is large and oval, ranging from 25 cm to 15 cm in length. The flowers are small and white, and grow from the spikes in the leaf axils near the ends of branches.
Location	Generally found growing near the coast in the subtropical woodlands of Western Australia and the Northern Territory.
Flavour	The taste is tart and bitter. It has the aroma of stewed apples and pears, with cooked citrus and fermented notes.
Health benefits	The Kakadu plum has the highest recorded levels of vitamin C in the world, and is the richest source of antioxidant compounds. It contains a rich mixture of phenolic compounds, and is a good source of vitamin E, folate and lutein. Also high in the essential minerals potassium, magnesium and calcium.
Uses	Traditionally, the Kakadu Plum was used both as food and in healing remedies. It can be used as an antiseptic and as a soothing balm for aching limbs. It's also an excellent source of a variety of vitamins and minerals.
	The fruit is good for jams, sauces, juices, ice-cream and deserts and is even used in cosmetics. Recently, Kakadu plum extract has been used to extend the shelf-life of fresh prawns.

MUNTRIES/MUNTARI/CRAB APPLE	
Botanical name	*Kunzea pomifera*
Description	Muntries grow on a shrub, which is found either slightly upright or, more generally, flattened against the ground. The berries are small, 8–12 mm, resembling tiny figs, and are a purple-green colour. They grow in small clusters near the end of the branches and are furry-skinned, with each one containing several small seeds. The leaves of the shrub are small and hard, growing thickly along each branch. The flowers are white, with small round petals.
Location	The shrub grows on the south coast of Australia, with inland extensions, from Portland in Victoria to the Eyre Peninsula and Kangaroo Island in South Australia. It is a woody creeper of coastal dunes. It can also be found in clearings of mallee and desert woodlands.
Flavour	Muntries are sweet and apple-flavoured, with an aroma of moist fruit mince, spice, honey and butter.
Health benefits	High in antioxidants
Uses	Perennially popular for use in jams, chutneys, pies, desserts, fruit salads, and sweet or savoury sauces

DESERT QUANDONG

Botanical name	*Santalum acuminatum*
Description	A shrub or small tree with long, olive-green leaves that resemble eucalyptus leaves and hang from the thin drooping stems. The fruit is the size of a 20 cent coin, resembling a fat avocado. The colour of its skin is a shiny red (occasionally yellow). Inside, as with an avocado, is a large stone and the flesh is found around it.
Location	Normally found in the bottom half of Australia, the desert quandong grows in woodlands, on stony soils and sand.
Flavour	The taste is acidic, tart and with a saltiness. Its aroma is of dry lentils or beans, with some earthy and fermented notes.
Health benefits	Very high in antioxidants; good source of vitamins C and E, and folate; extremely rich in magnesium, zinc and iron
Uses	The fruit is excellent in pies and jellies. They are also good dried. The kernel nut is also edible.

RIBERRY

Botanical name	*Syzygium leuhmannii*
Description	Riberry fruit is small – up to 13 mm long – and pear-shaped. Its colouring can range from bright pink to magenta and purple. However, when cooked these fade to pink. The tree can reach upwards of 30 m in the wild. Under cultivation, they are kept at around 5 to 10 m.
Location	Generally found in northern New South Wales, but also native to rainforests from Kempsey, New South Wales, to Cooktown in north-eastern Queensland. It has the potential to be grown in many other areas.
Flavour	The fruit is refreshingly tart, having a spicy sweet flavour of spiced tea, with musky notes and a hint of cloves, cinnamon and nutmeg often present.
Health benefits	100 g of riberries contains 50% of the recommended daily intake of folate; high in antioxidants and magnesium; good levels of calcium, vitamin E and manganese.
Uses	Works well in sauces and chutneys, and goes well with game meat, as well as poultry, pork and lamb. Can be used as you would a juniper berry (indeed, there is now a riberry gin). Also works in salads and desserts.

ANISE MYRTLE

Botanical name	*Syzygium anisatum*
Description	The tree, called either ringwood or aniseed, is a rainforest tree, often described as stunning and ornamental. It can reach up to 45 m in the rainforest environment, but most often it will grow to 8–10 m in open gardens. The plant has a dense cover of fine green foliage throughout the year and its white scented flowers blossom in spring. The 6–12 cm leaves release a strong aniseed aroma when crushed.
Location	Quite rare in the wild, native to a handful of areas of north-east New South Wales, primarily the Nambucca and Bellingen valleys.
Flavour	It has a taste of aniseed, sweet and cooling on the palate, and an aroma of menthol and aniseed.
Health benefits	High in antioxidants, vitamin E, lutein, magnesium and phenolics. Good source of Vitamins C and A, and zinc. Traditionally used for weight loss, to promote lactation and ease stomach complaints.
Uses	Often used for flavouring in desserts, sweet sauces and preserves. It is also popular in savoury sauces and marinades for meats and salad dressings. Also used in essential oils.

LEMON MYRTLE	
Botanical name	*Backhousia citriodora*
Description	Grows up to 3 m in height, with long hanging branches of soft green leaves, and clusters of cream flowers in autumn.
Location	Naturally occurring in wetter coastal areas of northern New South Wales and coastal rainforest areas 50–800 m above sea level in Queensland.
Flavour	It has an aroma of creamy lemon and lime, with notes of menthol. The flavour is like lemon candy – a strong lemon/lemongrass flavour and sweet, cooling on the palate.
Health benefits	High in antioxidants. Extremely high in calcium. High levels of magnesium, vitamin E and lutein.
Uses	Complements fish, chicken, ice-cream or sorbet. Its essential oils contain antimicrobial compounds and it is often used as an ingredient in shampoos, therapeutic body lotions, soaps and household cleaners.

BUSH TOMATO

Botanical name	*Solanum centrale*
Description	A small shrubby and prickly plant, which can grow anywhere from 15–100 cm tall, with grey-green furry leaves which have a velvet texture. The flowers are a purple/lavender colour with a yellow centre. The fruit turns from green to yellow when it ripens. When it is dried on the plant, it goes a reddish-ochre colour and resembles a raisin. The fruit contains many black seeds.
Location	The bush tomato is a desert plant, growing naturally through the central deserts from Tennant Creek, Northern Territory, to Marla, South Australia.
Flavour	The flavour has carob notes, and is mostly savoury with some sweetness.
Health benefits	Contains medium levels of antioxidants, vitamin E, zinc and calcium. Rich source of folate, magnesium, iron and potassium. Bush tomato is a source of selenium, which is necessary for antioxidant enzymes to function.
Uses	The bush tomato works well with cheese, eggs, salmon and stronger-flavoured white or game meats. It can also be used in dukka or crusting on meats. Can be eaten dried or fresh. Also used by Indigenous communities to treat toothaches.

TASMANIAN PEPPERBERRY

Botanical name	*Tasmannia lanceolata*
Description	Also known as mountain pepper, it grows on a bushy compact shrub that can grow from 2 to 10 m high. The leaves are thin, green and long, 5–20 cm, with wavy edges. The plants are either male or female. Both sexes have small cream-coloured flowers with narrow petals. The male flower has many stamens; the female flower has a two-lobed ovary. The berries grow in clusters, and can be coloured either a pinkish white or a purplish black, pea-sized with a deep furrow on one side.
Location	It can be found on rainforest edges and mountain eucalyptus forests, from Tasmania north to the Barrington Tops of New South Wales.
Flavour	The heat is between pepper and chilli, but much more complex. Almost fruit-candy sweet in both aroma and effect on the palate, but with a lingering heat.
Health benefits	High in folate, zinc, magnesium, manganese and antioxidants. Medium levels of iron. Polygodial, a compound found in the fruit and leaves, is antimicrobial and antifungal.
Uses	Used as a conventional pepper for preparing savouries, soups, vinaigrettes, pasta, meat, etc. Great with steak.

TASMANIAN PEPPER LEAF/MOUNTAIN PEPPER

Botanical name	*Tasmannia lanceolata*
Description	As above.
Location	As above.
Flavour	The aroma of dry paperbark, and herbal. A very intense heat on the palate, which develops slowly.
Health benefits	High in antioxidants, vitamin E, folate, magnesium, zinc, calcium, iron, lutein and provitamin A.
Uses	Can be added to olive oil for dressings, or used crumbled over soups and in sauces.

WATTLESEED/GUNDABLUIE/BARDI BUSH

Botanical name	*Acacia victoriae*
Description	A shrub-like tree with multiple trunks. The leaves are long and thin, the flowers small bulbous and yellow, the pods long, like a bean or carob pod.
Location	Can be found throughout the Central Desert region and into South Australia, Western Australia and New South Wales.
Flavour	A nutty flavour, with overtones of coffee and chocolate – a savoury flavour with some bitterness. An aroma of crushed nuts and cereal.
Health benefits	High in magnesium, zinc, iron. Medium levels of calcium and low levels of selenium. High in fibre.

WATTLESEED/GUNDABLUIE/BARDI BUSH (CONT.)

Uses	You can roast the wattleseed and turn it into a type of flour – this was done by the Aborigines. Some types can be eaten green or cooked in the pod. It can also be used to thicken sauces and casseroles, or even ice-cream. It can be dry-roasted and used as a beverage, or added to chocolate and desserts.

GREEN PLUM

Botanical name	*Buchanania obovata*
Description	A medium-sized plant, 4–10 m tall, that grows beneath other trees in woodlands native to northern Australia. The fruit is round and fleshy and around 2 cm long. It is smooth and green and resembles a small green mango. The flowers are small and cream-coloured, and around 0.5 cm across. The leaves are egg-shaped, thick and smooth, with a leathery feel. They are a dull green-grey colour, and can be anywhere between 5–25 cm long and 1–10 cm across.
Location	Found in upper north-west Australia, near the coast. Also in the Kimberley region and on the Queensland–Northern Territory border around Wollogorang.
Flavour	Highly aromatic, with a distinct taste, this plant is in the mango family.
Health benefits	Good source of vitamin C.
Uses	Used traditionally for ailments such as toothache. Often the entire fruit is pounded into a paste to be eaten.

WILD GRAINS

This is an area that has only recently been receiving scientific attention. There are some 1100 perennial grass species native to Australia. The seeds of many are edible and have been a part of the Indigenous diet for millennia. And, as Bruce Pascoe asks, 'What would happen if we tried some of the Aboriginal grains instead of the thirsty and disease-prone grains of Europe and Asia?'

An RIRDC report published in June of 2015, 'Native grasses make new products – a review of current and past uses and assessment of potential', is a first step in answering that question. I'll provide a link to that report in the Bibliography (see page 257; Chivers et al.) for anyone interested in reading the whole report. Below is a brief resume of a few of them. With all these native grain and grass species out there, and the foundations of research established, it can only be hoped that at least some of them will come on the market in the near future.

Wild rice

A number of species of plants in the genus *Oryza*, or rice, grow here. They were used by the Indigenous population and there is some small-scale production that makes it to local markets. As noted previously, Dr Penny Wurm of Charles Darwin University has been researching native rice for over twenty years. And Japanese breeders have undertaken cross-breeding programs with Asian (common) rice, *Oryza sativa*, to integrate some of the novel characteristics of the Australian rices. Once more we outsource the intellectual work, and perhaps lose control of a resource ...

Alpine rice

A close relative of the *Oryza* genus, *Microlaena stipoides* is the most advanced of the native grains, and is already on the market. It offers many benefits to the environment: it's deep-rooted, doesn't need to be replanted every season, doesn't require fertilisers, is well adapted to regular drought and low fertility soil, and can be used both as a grazing fodder and for grain production – it cooks like cultivated imported rice. Here is another example where it is hard to understand why this food is not more widely available and used. You'll find a link to an RIRDC report entitled 'Native grasses make new products – a review of current and past uses and assessment of potential' in the Bibliography.

Wild sorghums

Although more often used as crop feed, some of these were eaten by Indigenous people, and research on them is ongoing.

MEATS

The most commonly used native game meats are **kangaroo** and **wallaby**. The efforts of Paroo Premium Kangaroo have been recorded in chapter 7, 'The producers'. You can find their website – along with that of Lenah Games Meats, who market wallaby and, for those who want to try it, possum – in the next section, 'Useful contacts'. These sites will also give information on the best cuts and the best way of cooking them, as will some of the recipes in this book.

GAME BIRDS

If ever there was an example of a tragic waste of our natural resources, it is the disregard by non-Aboriginal Australians of the potential of native game birds: the **emu**, **Australian bustard**, **scrub (or bush or brush) turkey**, **Cape Barren goose** and **crested pigeon**. These are unique table birds that could be farmed lucratively or culled sustainably (as with the kangaroo and wallaby) and added to the national table. Take the scrub or bush turkey: instead of being bred for the table, they are seen as a pest.

Only two of them – magpie goose and emu – are being utilised at the time of writing, and magpie goose only just before this book went to print. And both are difficult to find. Nevertheless, I have listed those game birds which have a reputation for good flavour, in the hope that there may be some change. Who knows but that in the future other birds may find their way onto non-Indigenous tables.

I should also add that, if you are so inclined, you can hunt both the magpie goose and the Cape Barren goose in season, and of course there are seasons for duck and quail hunting in most states. There is considerable agitation against duck hunting. Surely it would be better to farm or sustainably cull them, using professional shooters, as is done for the kangaroo and wallaby.

USEFUL CONTACTS

aboriginalbushtraders.com Aboriginal Bush Traders is a not-for-profit initiative that assists with the development, retail and promotion of Indigenous products and services from around the Top End. Useful information, especially if you're planning a trip.

alpinerice.com.au Australia's first commercial native grain crop

anbg.gov.au/fungi/fungimap.html The FUNGIMAP project is an attempt to gather information on Australian fungi, which is very sparse. You can contribute.

anfil.org.au The peak body for Australian native food producers

astridsbushtucker.com An online shop for fresh and frozen and processed native foods

bushfoodsensations.net A clearing house for news, recipes, restaurants and much else about what they call bush tukka

cherikoff.net Pioneer Vic Cherikoff's retail site, which also contains a wealth of information on native foods

lenah.com.au Tasmanian game meats supplier, a source for wallaby

mayiharvests.com Ethical and sustainable Indigenous-owned native food company based in Broome. On this site you'll find two short videos on the savannah enrichment program.

outbackpride.com.au Mike and Gayle Quarmby's Australian native food supplier, which develops a network of production sites within traditional Aboriginal communities

outbackspirit.com.au Producers of a range of Australian native foods, also working in partnership with Aboriginal communities

parookangaroo.com.au Premium kangaroo supplier

BIBLIOGRAPHY

Books

Abbott, Edward A. (1864) *The English and Australian Cookery Book Cookery for the Many, As Well As for the Upper Ten Thousand*, republished as *The Colonial Cookbook* (1970), Paul Hamlyn, Dee Why

Archer, Michael and Beale, Bob (2004) *Going Native: Living in the Australian Environment*, Hodder, Sydney

Brand Miller, Janette, James, Keith W. and Maggiore, Patricia M. A. (1993) *Tables of Compositions of Aboriginal Foods*, Australian Institute of Aboriginal and Torres Strait Islander Studies, Canberra

Burarrwanga, Laklak and family (2013) *Welcome to My Country*, Allen & Unwin, Sydney

Clarke, Phillip A. (2014) *Discovering Aboriginal Plant Use: The Journeys of an Australian Anthropologist*, Rosenberg, Dural

Cowlishaw, Gillian and Morris, Barry (eds) (1997) *Race Matters: Indigenous Australians and 'Our' Society*, Aboriginal Studies Press, Canberra

Crosby, Alfred W. (1986) *Ecological Imperialism: The Biological Expansion of Europe, 900–1900*, Cambridge University Press, Cambridge

Davis, Stephen, *Man of All Seasons* (1989) Angus & Robertson, Sydney

Egan, Jack (1999) *Buried Alive: Sydney 1788–1792 Eyewitness Accounts of the Making of a Nation*, Allen & Unwin, Sydney

Gammage, Bill (2011) *The Biggest Estate on Earth: How Aborigines Made Australia*, Allen & Unwin, Sydney

Gould, Richard A. (1969) *Yiwara: Foragers of the Australian Desert*, Charles Scribner's Sons, New York

Isaacs, Jennifer (1992) *Bush Food: Aboriginal Food and Herbal Medicine*, Ure Smith, Sydney

Karskens, Grace (1999) *Inside The Rocks: The Archaeology of a Neighbourhood*, Hale & Iremonger, Sydney

Lévi-Strauss, Claude (1994) *The Raw and the Cooked*, Pimlico, US

Leichhardt, Ludwig, *Journal of an Overland Expedition in Australia, from Moreton Bay to Port Essington, a Distance of Upwards of 3000 Miles, During the Years 1844–1845*, <ebooks.adelaide.edu.au/l/leichhardt/ludwig/l52j/index.html>

Low, Tim (1992) *Wild Food Plants of Australia*, Angus & Robertson, Sydney

Newton, John (2009) *The Roots of Civilisation*, Murdoch Books, Sydney

Neidjie, Bill and Lang, Mark (2015) *Old Man's Story: The Last Thoughts of Kakadu Elder Bill Neidjie* (as told to Mark Lang), Aboriginal Studies Press, Canberra

Pascoe, Bruce (2014) *Dark Emu, Black Seeds: Agriculture or Accident?* Magabala Books, Broome

Probyn, Elspeth (2000) *Carnal Appetites: FoodSexIdentities*, Routledge, London

Roberts, Jonathan (2001) *The Origins of Fruit and Vegetables*, HarperCollins, London

Reynolds, Henry (2001) *An Indelible Stain?*, Viking, Ringwood, Vic.
——— (1998) *This Whispering in Our Hearts*, Allen & Unwin, Sydney

Rowse, Tim (1998) *White Flour, White Power*, Cambridge University Press, Melbourne

Seddon, George (2005) *The Old Country: Australian Landscapes, Plants and People*, Cambridge University Press, Melbourne

Stanner, W. E. H. (2009) *The Dreaming and Other Essays*, Black Inc. Agenda, Collingwood

Symons, Michael (2007) *One Continuous Picnic*, Melbourne University Press, Carlton

Turner, Margaret-Mary (1994) *Arrernte Foods: Foods from Central Australia*, IAD Press, Alice Springs

Walker, Kath [Oodgeroo Noonuccal] (1966) *The Dawn Is at Hand*, Jacaranda Press, Brisbane

Watson, Don (2014) *The Bush: Travels in the Heart of Australia*, Penguin, Melbourne

Journal articles and reports

Bannerman, C. (2006) 'Indigenous food and cookery books: redefining Aboriginal cuisine', *Journal of Australian Studies*, 30:87, 19–36, <dx.doi.org/10.1080/14443050609388048>

Brimblecombe, J., Maypilama, E., Colles, S., Scarlett, M., Dhurrka, J. G., Ritchie, J. and O'Dea, K. (2014) 'Factors influencing food choice in an Australian Aboriginal community' *Qualitative Health Research*, 24:387, originally published online 18 February 2014, <http://qhr.sagepub.com/content/24/3/387.full>

Cushing, N. (2014) 'Meat for the pot? Assessing animals in colonial Australia', paper presented at International Food Studies Conference, University of Adelaide, 18 February 2014.

Dunlap, T.R. (1997) 'Remaking the land: the acclimatization movement and Anglo ideas of nature', *Journal of World History*, 8:2, 303–19

Flowers, R. and Swan, E. (2012) 'Eating the Asian other? Pedagogies of food multiculturalism in Australia', *Journal of Multidisciplinary International Studies*, 9:2

Ishak, N., Salehuddin Mohd Zahari, M. and Othman, Z. (2013) 'Influence of acculturation on foodways among ethnic groups and common acceptable food', *Procedia – Social and Behavioral Sciences*, 105, 438–44

Konczak, I., Zabaras, B., Dunstan, M., Aguas, P., Roulfe, P. and Pavan, A. (2009) 'Health benefits of Australian native foods', RIRDC publication 09/133, <rirdc.infoservices.com.au/downloads/09-133>

Lee, A. J., Hobson, V. and Katarski, L. (1996) 'Review of the nutrition policy of the Arnhem Land Progress Association', *Australian and New Zealand Journal of Public Health*, 20, 538–44

Mohanty, S. and Cock, I. (2012) 'The chemotherapeutic potential of *Terminalia ferdinandiana*: phytochemistry and bioactivity', *Pharmacognosy Reviews*, 6:11, 29–36.

Chivers, I., Warrick, R., Bornman, J. and Evans, C. (2015) 'Native grasses make new products – a review of current and past uses and assessment of potential', RIRDC, <rirdc.infoservices.com.au/items/15-056>

Netzel, M., Netzel, G., Tian, Q. and Konczak, I. (2007) 'Native Australian fruits – a novel source of antioxidants for food', *Innovative Food Science and Emerging Technologies*, 8, 339–46

Newell, D. (2012) 'A fork in the road', *Griffith Review* 37, <griffithreview.com/articles/a-fork-in-the-road/>

Pedersen, A. and Walker, Iain (1997) 'Prejudice against Australian Aborigines: old-fashioned and modern forms', *European Journal of Social Psychology*, 27, 561–87

Santich, B. (2011) 'Nineteenth-century experimentation and the role of Indigenous foods in Australian food culture', *Australian Humanities Review*, 51

Singley, B. (2012) '"Hardly anything fit for Man to eat": food and colonialism in Australia', *History Australia*, 9:3, 27–42

Smith, P. A. and Smith, R. M. (1999) 'Diets in transition: hunter-gatherer to station diet and station diet to the self-select store diet', *Human Ecology*, 27:1, 115–33

Soukoulis, L. (1990) 'Black gift, white commodity', *Meanjin*, 49:2, 263–69

Wacquant, L. (2011) 'Habitus as topic and tool: reflections on becoming a prizefighter', *Qualitative Research in Psychology*, 8:1, 81–92, <loicwacquant.net/assets/Papers/HABITUSASTOPICTOOL-QRP.pdf>

Online

Aboriginal Bush Traders, <www.aboriginalbushtraders.com>

Australian Native Food Industry (ANFIL), <www.anfil.org.au>

Brain, C. (2014), 'Researchers go wild for Australian native rice', ABC Rural, 16 May, <www.abc.net.au/news/2014-05-15/native-australian-wild-rice-indigenous/5455764>

Cameron-Smith, B. (1987) *Starting from Scratch: Australia's First Farm*, Royal Botanic Gardens, Sydney, <www.rbgsyd.nsw.gov.au/welcome/royal_botanic_garden/gardens_and_domain/feature_gardens/first_farm/_nocache>

Central Australian Aboriginal Congress, <caac.org.au>

Clarke, M. (2012), *Australian Native Food Industry Stocktake*, <rirdc.infoservices.com.au/items/12-066>

Darwin, C. (1845), *The Voyage of the Beagle*, <literature.org/authors/darwin-charles/the-voyage-of-the-beagle/>

Rural Industries Research and Development Corporation (2008), *The New Crop Industries Handbook: Native Foods*, RIRDC, <rirdc.infoservices.com.au/downloads/08-021.pdf>

Thomas, A. (2010), 'Native rice may hold key to food future', ABC Science, 15 October, <abc.net.au/science/articles/2010/10/15/3038568.htm>

The Voyage of Governor Phillip to Botany Bay (compilation), <gutenberg.net.au/ebooks/e00101.html#chapter-08>

ACKNOWLEDGMENTS

This book began life as one part of my doctoral thesis at the University of Technology, Sydney. So I must first acknowledge my debt to Professor Paul Ashton, my supervisor, who led me through the thorny forests of academia to eventual success.

The next person I'd like to acknowledge is the young Aboriginal bloke, whose name I have forgotten, who was in my class when I was teaching a Creative Thinking class at Billy Blue School of Graphic Design in the 1990s. He'd been playing for a rugby league club in England, had come back to Australia and received a scholarship to Billy Blue. We struck up a sort of a master/pupil friendship.

One day he walked up to me after class and thrust a book at me. 'Read this,' he said, and walked away. The book was *Pemulwuy: The Rainbow Warrior*, by Eric Willmot. Put simplistically – and it is a long time since I read it – it's the story of an Aboriginal warrior who conducts guerrilla warfare on the invaders of his land.

When I had just finished the book I had to go, for some reason, to Elizabeth Bay House, built in the 1830s and known as 'the finest house in the colony'. As I entered this grand and imposing neoclassical mansion, it struck me hard for the first but not the last time that it had been built on land that had been stolen from people who had, most likely, been murdered, or at the very least marginalised. That book changed my perspective on being Australian.

I want to thank the chefs (and their publishers) who gave of their time, recipes and their stories: Jean-Paul Bruneteau, Laklak Burarrwanga, Beau Clugston, Raymond and Jennice Kersh, Phillip Searle, Peter Gilmore, Maggie Beer, Tony Bilson, Clayton Donovan, Kylie Kwong, Andrew Fielke, Simon Bryant, Matt Stone, Mark Olive, and, posthumously, Chris Jackman.

To all the producers and suppliers for their stories. And to Amanda Garner of ANFIL, who seems to know everyone involved in this vast enterprise, right across the country. Her introductions were invaluable.

And Phillipa McGuinness and NewSouth Publishing, who had the courage and, I believe, the foresight to publish this book.

I must also thank the wonderful people – Blackfellas and Whitefellas – I met and talked with while writing this book. People who told me stories of survival, hard yakka, creativity and persistence in the face of indifference.

It looks like they might finally be winning.

INDEX

Page numbers in **bold** indicate recipes. Those in *italics* refer to charts and illustrations. Full titles of recipes appear under the heading 'recipes'.

Index

Index

Index